Mary-
Thank you for [illegible] Support.
Love [illegible]
(Thomas)
6/2020

Blessed NOT BROKEN

JOURNEY TO FINDING PURPOSE
IN MARRIAGE, MOTHERHOOD & ENTREPRENEURSHIP
AS A CEO WIFE

FOREWORD BY LUCINDA CROSS-OTITI

NEW YORK TIMES BEST SELLING AUTHOR OF ***THE BIG ASK***

Blessed NOT BROKEN

JOURNEY TO FINDING PURPOSE
IN MARRIAGE, MOTHERHOOD & ENTREPRENEURSHIP
AS A CEO WIFE

VISIONARY AUTHOR

TAMARA MITCHELL-DAVIS

Blessed Not Broken: Journey to Finding Purpose in Marriage, Motherhood & Entrepreneurship as a CEO Wife

Published by CEO Wife Publishing
www.theceowife.com

Manuscript Editing
Robin R. Ashworth, Ph.D
www.linkedin.com

Book Creation and Design
DHBonner Virtual Solutions, LLC
www.dhbonner.net

ISBN for Paperback: 978-1-7328270-4-2
ISBN for E-Book: 978-1-7328270-5-9
Library of Congress Control Number: 2020907983

Printed in the United States of America

This book is dedicated to the women who have questioned their worth, paused on pursuing their purpose, and doubted their gifts, abilities and talents. We are rooting for you.

Delayed doesn't mean denied. May you be inspired and impacted by the stories you read and the co-authors you connect with.

#everyonehasastorytotell | #BlessedNotBroken

Table of Contents

Foreword

Lucinda Cross-Otiti

What is a CEO Wife?

When I look at the title of this book, I reflect on what I think a CEO wife is. With all the roles we play in life, we are constantly graduating and adding more responsibilities to our plates, and more notches to our professional belts. We collect titles with each achievement and experience: the woman, the lover, the friend, the mother, the nurturer, the supporter, the sister-friend, the career woman, the visionary, the wife, and the wealth creator.

The CEO Wife creates a life of wealth, health, happiness and love for her circle. She is also known as the Proverbs 31 woman. But how does a woman come to recognize this in herself? Is it a feeling, something to be measured, a belief, a practice? Is there a secret, a series of steps, 101 keys, or 40 days and 40 nights of process? Is a CEO Wife potentially every woman, or only the elected? Is a CEO Wife based on color, or creed, nationality, or religion?

These are questions I am sure you will have answered upon reading the wise counsel from other powerful women who can rightfully call themselves 'CEO Wife' in this purpose driven anthology journey. In my experience as a CEO Wife, the role and the position of success is defined on my own terms. To me, the CEO Wife is formed through loving relationships, mindful health, a lifestyle that cultivates opportunities, time with family, and a heartfelt acknowledgement of simple things that life gives us for free.

THE W IN WIFE STANDS FOR WORTH

There is a price to be paid for everything you do and don't do. Self-worth is one of the streets we all must travel down whether we like it or not. When you look at your life and you look at your business, how are you showing up in the world? Are you presenting yourself with a symbol of worthiness? It is so important to mean what you say and say what you mean. It is equally important to have a powerful YES and a strong NO.

In society, I see how people are getting physically sick every day by doing something they don't want to do, going to a job they don't like, and staying in unhealthy relationships that tear them down mentally and emotionally. I have been there and done that and have the t-shirt and mug to prove it. You have got to start feeling WORTHY. Start by practicing saying YES. Yes, to your life, yes to your future, and yes to your potential.

Repeat after me:

This is my season; I declare this is my season. I am worthy to be free. I am worthy to be loved. And I am worthy to be wealthy.

THE I IN WIFE STANDS FOR INSPIRATION

Inspiration is what will motivate you to create and operate in the bigger picture. You must accept an ongoing shift in your psyche that focuses on your inspirational value. Don't worry about the background singers, the inner conversations that tell you that you can't, or that you are too short, too tall, too light, too dark, too educated, too uneducated, too this, or too that.

You must activate your own power of inspiration in order to create your own economy, support your community, and make $$$ in your pajamas. The CEO Wife comes in many forms and if you continue to abandon your inspirational power you will never fully step into your full potential.

What happens to us many times is that we get satisfied and we procrastinate. Not feeling worthy of your goal will cause you to have distractions. Complaining and never looking for an outcome or solution, just looking at the current situations will cause you to never do anything but sit there. The most exciting thing about being inspirational – and being inspired – is that you understand you have greatness in you. You have talents and skills that no one else has. The thing that makes me sad is that many of you are not willing to sacrifice in order to be fruitful.

THE F IN WIFE STANDS FOR FRUITFUL

As a CEO Wife I had to go through stages of sacrifices to stretch past stereotypes, ridicule, and lack of support in order to speak my truth and stand in my power. For me to believe in myself when no one else believed. For me to invest when no one else would invest. It meant that I needed to plant seeds and replant seeds based on reasons and seasons in my life. I want you to remember this and write it down:

You don't get in life what you want,
you get what and who you are.

Regardless of my position or situation as a CEO Wife, that did not change my gifts, talents, skills or abilities. Regardless of my position it did not define me or limit me from being worthy, inspirational or fruitful even in my moments of limitations.

This leads me to my final point as you press forward to read the rest of this amazing book. Get a firm anchor as to why you are doing what you are doing and defining your purpose and mission. The point in this search is to find a big enough reason WHY. This will help you determine what you need to do next. Never worry about the how, you just focus on the what.

THE E IN WIFE STANDS FOR EXCELLENCE

I had to oftentimes ask myself: *Lucinda, who do you need to be? What do you need to do in order to have the life you deserve and desire?*

I want you to take two steps today. One, I want you to decide what you intend to create. Two, I want you to believe you deserve to have the best and live the best according to your divine purpose.

Here are some more questions to consider:

- What brings you joy?
- What makes your heart melt?
- What do you want to be in business for?
- What does wealth look like to you?

As you operate in excellence, you must stay hungry; you must understand you are pregnant with power. You will have cravings for information. You are going to be stretched, and you are going to be uncomfortable. This is a part of the necessary process you must go through in order to grow through who you are destined to be. A change-maker, a challenger, a visionary... the best darn CEO Wife that God has ever created.

God has gifted you with the power to persevere, to overcome, to transform, to love, to give, to stand. Use your CEO Wife power of Worth, Inspiration, Fruitfulness, and Excellence to get what's yours.

As women and wives, we do it all, for everyone, everywhere, however, whenever, for whomever, but the one person who needs it most. We believe that the more we give of ourselves, the better we will feel, being a better mom, wife, follower, steward, sister, daughter, etc. This is far from the truth. Your experiences are about you valuing your self-worth, your power, your mystery, and your divinity. It's the organic essence of who you've been, who you are not, who you want to be and who you are right now.

I am honored to write the foreword of this book that serves as a guide. By the time you finish reading this book, I guarantee you are going to begin to reap your harvest from all the work you put in, the growing up you had to do, the tears you shed, the healing and wound licking you had to do, the sleepless nights with just you and God, the speaking of truth, and the telling of lies to protect. You are going to press forward completing this assignment with a new pep in your step.

Lucinda Cross-Otiti
Author of NY Times Best Seller ***The Big ASK***
TV Personality/ Lifestyle Business Consultant
President of **Activate Worldwide**

IG: @lucindacross
FB: @lucindacrossspeaks
Web: www.lucindacross.com

The Quest for Something More

Tamara Mitchell-Davis

"'For I know the plans I have for you,' declares the Lord, ' plans to prosper you and not to harm you, plans to give you hope and a future.'"

~ Jeremiah 29:11 (NIV)

I remember, as I was building my business, a conversation I had with a potential client. I asked her to tell me a little bit about herself, and her immediate response was, "I am a broke wife." That statement made the hairs on my arms stand up. My thoughts went into overdrive, and I wanted her to tell me more about being a broke wife because those words resonated with me. How had this become her narrative? Was she okay with her feelings, or even the words that came out of her mouth?

Because we were talking about business, I automatically assumed she meant broke financially, but as we talked more, some real and raw things surfaced. She felt unappreciated, lost, and without a sense of purpose at work and in her marriage. She shared with me how life seemed to be filled with loss, heartache, and challenges. We talked for quite a while, and I encouraged her as best I could to keep pushing, to find hope in what she felt was a hopeless situation, and to pray about the things that were happening to her, and even her reaction to them. That was my automatic response because that's what I had been conditioned and taught to do. As far back as elementary school days, there were certain principles that I remembered: help others, give and you shall receive, and, of course, be kind.

As we hung up the phone, I sat on the couch and recalled our entire conversation word for word, assessing the advice I had given, while also assessing my own space and capacity with the word 'broke.' I wondered how long she had been feeling this way. As I dissected and considered the word further, that's when truth hit me, and I connected heart to heart with a woman who identified as a "broke" wife.

After one failed marriage, bankruptcy, and a ton of other losses, I could definitely identify with her feelings of brokenness. I am here to tell you my first divorce was my darkest and lowest point. I'd never felt so humiliated, abandoned, unworthy, and rejected in my life until that moment in time.

Financially or otherwise, feelings of inadequacy, hopelessness, worthlessness, and loss can show up at any given time in various aspects of our lives. We may find ourselves struggling with work, household, business, relationships, self-esteem, and confidence at any point in time. And often, the conditioned responses we are taught to offer ourselves and others do nothing to solve that brokenness. And so, I began to question myself, my patterns, my way of thinking, my conditioning. How could I change that narrative?

What could I do to make sure those I worked with would avoid those same words and feelings?

For me, this became a quest to figure out the 'secret sauce' so other women and wives like me wouldn't feel limited and broke financially, emotionally, mentally and creatively. It was a sudden reminder for me as I flashed backed to different situations, challenges, and obstacles when I may have uttered those same words. If not 'broke wife,' then perhaps 'broke mom,' or 'broke woman.'

Prior to my current marriage, and even prior to starting my business, my mind was so polluted from inconsistencies. Inconsistencies with people in my life, broken promises, and even inconsistency with me showing up for myself. I developed a hard exterior to protect myself from anything that I thought would harm me. Some might say I was good at building walls, or that I was introverted or stand-offish. I liked to think I carried a shield. You know the shield of protection. I was trying to protect myself from people and things to avoid additional hurt, harm, danger, and the feeling of being broke.

As a single parent, I remember working jobs that I hated. I had no choice but to keep going because the paycheck helped to pay the bills to keep a roof over our heads, lights on, and food on the table. I was also broke emotionally. I dreaded going in to work, and even though I was pushing through to punch a clock, I left feeling unappreciated, undervalued, and mishandled regarding the number of hours I expended every day, every evening, and even the weekends. All for the sake of earning a paycheck. I was a robot, and the momentum and excitement of life escaped me. I found myself numb, existing but not living.

Oftentimes, I would sit and wonder what the hell was wrong with me? Why couldn't I get my shit together? There I was, a grown woman with a failed marriage and two children starting all over at ground zero. Job, empty apartment, new school, new town, government assistance, and having to find a new church home, and even new friends.

Starting my business was one of the best things I ever did for myself. Despite the risks of entrepreneurship, I felt a sense of control, freedom, and safety by working hard and building it up. I also leaned on my education and trusted my instincts and my work ethic. And I managed a comeback. I was also blessed with a second marriage to a man who supported my efforts.

We had sought pre-marital counseling, and I laid everything on the table to my husband. He knew what I was going through, had gone through, and what my plans were for the future. Even so, things weren't perfect. My husband never stopped or deterred me from pursuing the things I wanted. I was comfortable sharing ideas with him, but I sometimes felt there was a disconnect between us; he would listen, but I wouldn't always get the response I was looking for, or even an assessment or processing of ideas or information that I longed for. He was present, but I still felt alone.

We struggled with being on the same page, which in turn resulted in a lack of communication. And as I poured more and more of my time into the business, I began to realize that distance was becoming more and more common. We were like two ships passing in the night, leaving the house early in the morning, with no guarantee of seeing each other later in the evening. He didn't openly complain, but one night as I was working late in my office, he stopped by en route to bed and asked how long I would be. I told him only a few more minutes. A few minutes turned into hours, and by the time I went to bed, he was asleep.

The next day, as we were talking, he expressed his complete support of me, but asked me not to forget about him. Here I was thinking because I was pursuing my goals, cooking dinner, being intimate, and answering the phone every time he called, I was fulfilling my role as a wife. And yet, I was somehow missing the mark. We both were physically present for the most part, but struggling with balance to stay emotionally and mentally connected. I needed to have a hard talk with myself and assess my patterns, because I never wanted my husband or children to feel neglected or abandoned. My sense of fulfillment, success, and financial security, while certainly positive, had somehow eclipsed my partnership.

Entrepreneurship can cause division in a marriage just like so many other factors. If you dedicate an enormous amount of time to one thing over another, then predictably, some aspect of your life will not have as much of your attention. I didn't want to repeat my past, but I didn't have a model to emulate either. So, there I was trying to figure out how to have the best of both worlds: a strong, loving marriage, and a strong, sustained business.

As a wife, mom, and business owner, I've made some costly mistakes, but thankfully the mistakes didn't take me out. That's where resilience comes in, because I could have easily walked away, and given in to the pressure of it all, but I remained – and remained teachable. The learning and joy far outweighed the mishaps. I also took the time to figure out what my particular gifts were, as well as my shortcomings. And that wasn't easy.

Sometimes, life itself causes us to suppress our inherent talents, because we are in survival mode, or other priorities and relationships take precedence. I know my gift is strategy. It's like once an idea hits me, or someone presents a problem, I can come up with a million and one ways on how to solve it.

I also started thinking about my husband and children more carefully. I came to regard them as my team and recognized that we each were part of a much more important whole, regardless of our individual goals and desires. I made sure I was communicating clearly and fairly. I allowed myself to become transparent and vulnerable with them.

My husband continued to support me in word and deed. Whenever I had book signings or speaking engagements, he would be right there with me. So, I knew I had to reciprocate. If there were things he was pursuing, I would share my advice, but I wouldn't influence or pressure him to change his ideas. I made sure I showed up and supported him as he did the same for me.

I believe there is a way to support each other's dreams without feeling diminished. All relationships are different, and learning takes time. Balancing business and marriage has taught me nothing is perfect. There are good days and some not so great days. There are days when you are questioning if the effort is worth it, and grasping for answers, and then days when you know without a shadow of a doubt it's all worth it, and the answers are crystal clear. And let me confess that there were times when I made some poor decisions investing in people and services. But I've also made some great decisions by investing in personal and professional development for myself, my marriage, and my business. Marriage isn't easy, and neither is entrepreneurship, but I believe each is worth working for.

In Blessed, Not Broken, you will find stories of resilience, forgiveness, loss, determination, enlightenment, and perseverance told by several women, many of them wives, who experienced heartaches, challenges, hardships, obstacles, stages of growth, and bouts of brokenness in various areas of their lives.

To build on Lucinda's beautiful anagram, I would humbly add the 'F' in 'w-i-f- e' also stands for 'faithful.' Faithful not only to a marriage partner, but faithful to God, faithful to His vision, and faithful to oneself in fulfilling purpose. Open your heart and mind to receive the messages these women share about how they found hope and purpose through it all.

Peace and Blessings,
Tamara Mitchell-Davis
CEO & Visionary Author

Faith Kept It Together

Dr. Sh'nai Simmons

"And we know [with great confidence] that God [who is deeply concerned about us] causes all things to work together [as a plan] for good for those who love God, to those who are called according to His plan and purpose."
~ Romans 8:28 (AMP)

I was born to single parents, each with backgrounds saturated in trauma and addiction. My childhood and adolescent years were spent in the heart of the crack epidemic. My mom and dad separated when I was six months old, and I initially lived with my mom. My dad would surface from time to time for special occasions or to discipline me when my mom sent for him. As I grew, my mother's addiction worsened, and my behavior became uncharacteristic. I got into fights almost daily. I avoided the house and I became a bit disrespectful. My grandmother called for my father to come and intervene. He eventually came and invited me to live with him for the last time. He had asked me a few times prior, but I always declined. I was torn between wanting an escape from my mother's addiction and demonstrating loyalty to her and my siblings. But I was finally able to muster up the courage to choose me. I was only thirteen years old, and while it was a painful decision, I knew it was necessary.

I would soon realize the complexities of that decision. I had no clue my father was just as vulnerable to the same addiction my mother had. But his addiction and related behaviors were cloaked by my very committed stepmother. These realities would eventually fire up a desire for me to make sense of a world ensnaring my loved ones in such a fierce relationship with drugs. I was motivated to continue to look for a safe place to retreat, and I found that in my education.

Always an intelligent young girl, academics came easily for me. Consequently, I would lean on my accelerated school success as a salve for the pain of my childhood. As a freshman in high school, I attended multiple college fairs and was intently conversing with admissions representatives about my future.

After graduating high school, I moved to Buffalo, NY, for college, where I met the man who would become my amazing husband. We connected initially on a superficial level, but I'll save those details for another story. We learned that we had both come from similar backgrounds. While our stories were different, the same themes were evident in both our lives, and we quickly found friendship and deep understanding in one another.

At that time, I was concentrating on school, but I always had a major goal in mind. Shortly after I decided to move in with my father, my siblings were removed from my mother's home and placed in foster care. I felt responsible, so I vowed that as soon as I was 18 years old, I would seek custody of them. That was a non- negotiable goal. I made sure my boyfriend understood that as soon as it was clear that we would become an item. I was a focused young woman with no time for foolishness. So, while it felt good to have a beau in my first year of college, he needed to know that anyone serious about spending his life with me would be getting a package deal. I came with children, my three siblings. If that was not scary enough for a boyfriend to reckon with, he also had to be or help me become financially stable enough to get them out of foster care.

Well, my boyfriend agreed. He never complained or balked about the required commitment, which was quite a shock to me. He was accustomed to people coming into his home as his great-grandmother, who raised him, had often taken children in during his childhood. He would join the fight with me to convince the Bureau of Child Welfare (BCW) in New York City that we were equipped to care for my siblings. And so, our journey as fight buddies started in 1995, even before we were married.

We did get married in Buffalo City Hall in 1996, not long after becoming kinship foster parents for the kids, and only one month after losing our first-born son. A few of our family members were in attendance, and my siblings served as our wedding party. We were young, naive, excited, and motivated to tackle the world, though we were not entirely clear what that would look like. All we knew was that we would face it all together.

Neither of us had completed our degrees when we successfully adopted two of my three siblings. However, we had to maintain financial stability while we were still under surveillance by the foster care placement agency, which was monitoring our parenting. In our early twenties with three children to support, my husband was always open to listening to pitches to make more money. One revenue stream that continuously found us was multi-level marketing (MLM). I was never really interested in that avenue because it reminded me of the hustling my father did when I was a child. One time, my dad tried to make me sell spices and extracts after he had signed up for an MLM. However, my husband felt different about MLMs. He saw potential. He saw wealth. He saw freedom.

One day, as a newlywed couple struggling financially, we were presented an opportunity that caught my attention. This company was positioning itself to capitalize on the internet age, and there seemed to be a once-in-a-lifetime chance available. I agreed to participate this time, and I was committed to it. I not only consumed the products, but I learned how to become a businesswoman.

We traveled along the southeast coast, building our business and toting our family along with us. By this point, I had two of my own biological children and was highly motivated to figure out how to be a godly wife and mom. I was fortunate to encounter many good examples throughout our business activity. The people in our upline, and their affiliates, were not only living their values, but they were teaching them as well. We were learning how to be a team. We were learning how to be entrepreneurs. We were learning how to keep our faith at the core of all our efforts. We were encouraged to develop ourselves as individuals and as a married couple. We watched diligently, as we had always been desperate for successful marriage examples.

Ironically, I had not considered myself a full-time entrepreneur. I enjoyed the experience, but I was focused on making sure I finished school. An uncle had suggested that getting married would hinder that, so I had something to prove. And that is exactly what I did.

After I completed my undergraduate education, I got an advanced degree in counseling and a terminal degree in Counselor Education and Supervision.

When I completed my doctorate in 2011, I wasted no time sending the announcement to my uncle. By that time in my life, my husband and I had navigated many obstacles as a team. There were in-law squabbles, lay-offs, deaths, church hurt, and broken marital trust, just to name a few. We had developed a cohesion that was phenomenal, but it was time for me to define what my career path would be. I knew I wanted to be in a dynamic position, but no opportunity presented itself.

This was more than a little unsettling and scary if I'm being totally truthful. I would have to define my next step for myself, but I had no blueprint to follow. We had done everything as a team, but now I was venturing into uncharted territory. My husband was in the insurance industry, not counseling, so he was not able to lead the way for me this time. I found temporary refuge in my employment. I worked for a number of companies while accruing the hours needed to satisfy my licensure requirements, but I held my aspirations close to my heart.

Once I successfully acquired my license, my husband and I relocated to Florida with our pastor for a church plant. In our new location, we were excited and inspired as we declared new things were destined to come to us. We found work and began life, but our lives were met with one of the biggest obstacles yet. I was diagnosed with Stage III breast cancer.

I could not believe it! Life as I knew it changed instantly. I had never really been sick beyond a sinus infection, and maybe I got the flu once. This was mind-blowing.

Because we moved over 800 miles away from our primary support system, we found ourselves relying on God in a much more substantial way. In being challenged with this terrifying ordeal, I consulted my children's godmother, my spiritual big sister, who was also a three-time breast cancer survivor. She gave me the guidance I needed, along with practical tips about nutrition and energy conservation. She warned me to manage my emotions and stay focused on the healing power of God versus the ignorance of people who occasionally missed the mark in their interactions with me.

In addition to the guidance, one of her warnings served as the inspiration that keeps me going today. She explicitly told me not to put my dreams down. As a result, while working full-time and getting aggressive cancer treatment, I signed the lease for my very first office space and started my private practice. I had no clue what I was doing, but I incorporated my business and registered with the county as a licensed mental health counselor.

My fight for life against cancer was not an easy one; my strength was limited, my body image was impaired, and I questioned aspects of my sexuality. The treatment made it a serious challenge to be intimate with my husband. I wanted to connect with him. I wanted to be one with him, but it was physically too uncomfortable. There was no warning about this. I felt blind-sided. Even though I received absolutely no pressure from him, I felt inadequate as a woman, and this hijacked my emotions for a little while, as I had not even had breast surgery yet.

While all of this was physically challenging, the hardest part of the battle was in my mind. I questioned everything I knew. I questioned everything I wanted. I questioned everything I put my hands to do. I could not grasp why, after I had already overcome so much hardship, I would find myself in this space. In a moment of desperate supplication, I heard God reply to me, "Your life is not your own." Instantly, I had a very different lens through which I viewed my place in the world.

The experience of working for other companies and being vulnerable to their interpretation of my value was also painful. We had one too many instances in which our financial security was in the hands of someone deciding to "go in a different direction." The feeling of being dispensable was getting old. I found myself in a job with a bully for a supervisor, whose approach to service delivery was riddled with a bias toward one demographic.

I questioned her ethics and the ethos she was creating within the agency. She never hesitated to inconvenience me and could not have cared less about any aspect of my well-being. She barely consoled me when my grandmother and uncle passed within six months of one another. She suspiciously questioned any follow-up cancer treatment I had. She delayed my mileage reimbursement for reasons no one else under her leadership experienced. She relocated my office to a part of town, requiring me to spend an extra hour each day in traffic. She forced me to increase my direct service delivery time by 300%. I was miserable daily, and I needed an avenue to exit. That experience incited a passion in me to create a new space for myself in the industry.

After deciding to launch full-time into private practice, the exit strategy I had was perfected by God, and I was let go with severance pay. This was initially hard to accept, because I felt it was rooted in evil. The day I returned to work from medical leave, for reconstructive surgery, I was "allowed to resign." The irony was that I had already decided to resign while I was on medical leave. However, the conflict I had was figuring out how to do that with integrity. I had planned to wait for 30 days to see if things would improve at work. I was doubtful but that was the plan. My husband was quiet in the process. He made it clear that I needed to be the one to make that decision. He would not allow me to lean on him for this one. Well, as God would have it the job gave me the push. Once I got over my wounded pride, I embraced the liberty I was always looking for, and got busy. I began to use the skills I had learned early in my twenties through network marketing. I started shaking hands in the community. I was open for God's leading, and my husband gave me the space and encouragement to do that.

During the first year of my professional independence, we agreed I would get familiar with the landscape of the county in which we resided. I had to abide by a non-compete agreement, so I could not capitalize on the relationships I had made through my previous employment. Doors were opened for me in our county, and things moved quickly. We had moved our office twice and were given an opportunity to have a satellite office in a second location. The journey was exciting and terrifying at the same time as things became more complex. Although I had offices, I only went to them when a client was scheduled. Otherwise, I worked from home. It became easy to get lost in business planning and harder to account for my time. I was home, but I was not really engaged in home affairs. There were more days than I like to admit with no dinner prepared.

My children were pretty self- sufficient at this point, so it made it easier not to prioritize meal prep and other home maintenance. And, thankfully, my husband never really made much of a fuss.

Please do not get me wrong. My husband is not a saint. I do not want it to seem as if I only see him through rose-tinted lenses. While biblical love requires that to some degree, we have had tough moments. During the season of learning to embrace entrepreneurship for myself, his comments about my lack of balance often forced me to evaluate my own efficiencies. He would explain what he would like me to pay closer attention to and left it alone. We had committed to meet each other's needs when an issue surfaced, so I endeavored to figure it out. Our marriage has always been prioritized in our lives, second only to our personal walks with the Lord. We chose to place our children on the third rung of our lives' ladder, and our careers were fourth. By doing so, I developed the muscle of being more introspective.

I knew that I was high maintenance in ways that are not typical. I did not require a great number of material things; however, I required our family life to look a certain way to the public. We both had to be visible in our children's academic lives. My husband was often dad and coach, while also serving as tutor and housekeeper during my extended school years. I knew that had tried my husband's last nerve tremendously, well before cancer. I required a level of transparency in our marriage that was not modeled to us.

I wanted to be pampered by my husband, but allowed to be independent. I have a history of being overbearing and demanding. I had a lot of questions about what it meant to be a wife. Was that realistic? Is the Proverbs 31 woman some archaic, culturally misplaced mode pressuring women and convincing them that they are not enough? I was occasionally tempted to compare myself to the Proverbs 31 woman. Am I capable? Do I fully have my husband's trusting heart? What time is the right time to start the day? I am not innately kind, so what do I do about that?

I eventually learned the importance of rejecting comparisons. What I learned was the need to get out of my head about the matter and get the facts from my husband. How was I doing? What did he need me to attend to differently? How did he feel about our relationship as a whole? What were his expectations of me in the season we were in? Since we developed the practice of maintaining open lines of communication, we used that to navigate the challenges of the journey.

Although I was self-employed, I was not in business alone. We parented together. We served in ministry together. We served within our community together. We never did anything in total isolation, so my being in business would be no different.

Using the tools that reinforced our marriage also helped to reinforce my pursuit of entrepreneurship. We kept God's leading at the forefront of all our efforts. We talked openly about where we were. . . and where we wanted to be. We maintained our friendship with one another. We made the journey fun whenever possible, because it was already hard. We owned our own space in the process. Yes, we have different lanes, and the better we learned who we each were individually, the easier it was to complement one another in our efforts. I walk in the space of visionary for Community Victory Family Services. My husband is the operations leader. I handle the hearts of the people we serve. He handles the processes for the people we serve. From time to time, we experience some head butting, but because our functions are clearly defined, we find our way to resolution fairly quickly.

If I delve deeper into the intricacies of becoming an entrepreneur while being a Christian wife and honoring traditional gender roles, the reality is my greatest challenge was never my husband. He has always been my greatest cheerleader. Whatever challenge I have faced, even this specific book project, he has never questioned my capacity. He has never discouraged me. My husband has always pushed me to leap. His faith in the God in me has always pushed me to dig a little deeper.

While I tease that I am the smarter one in the family, it is without debate that my husband is our faith leader. His faith at one point was annoying because it felt just out of reach, but I am grateful that he stays the course. Because of my husband's faith, I have developed my own more intentionally. I had to have my own beyond the fight against cancer. I realized I could not survive on his in the long term.

As I grew my faith, I also had to tackle my own insecurities. I truly had to see my husband's contributions as complementary. There were times during which I felt frustrated by our different perspectives. I had to come to terms with my actual knowledge base and recognize what areas of my life were actual threats and liabilities to the lifespan of my business. I had to let go of the fact that I really had no clue about the necessary business mechanics for my vision and develop a plan for remedying that deficit.

Part of that plan included using my husband's strengths to bolster my business efforts. Where there was the potential to compete, we resisted. Another huge part of the plan was recognizing that there were plenty of good examples to follow, and we did not need to waste effort creating a new template. I had the distinct pleasure of having lunch with a pioneer in the breast cancer awareness movement in 2018. During that meeting, one of the most profound things she said to me was not to tell myself the lie that there was no one I could use as a mentor. She challenged me to look at things differently. She challenged me to humble myself and pursue people who could serve as mentors to me. I am forever grateful for that lesson. It was a necessary correction.

Today, as we venture into expanding the scope of our business, and take on larger risks, I am happy to share that I feel balanced for the first time ever. The road here has been interesting but what I can say is that it was worth it. On the way here, I learned that faith fuels any fight I face. I learned that I have a lifelong partner, and I do not have to do it all alone. I learned that I can take good care of myself, and my family, with some clear intention, preparing, and planning. I learned that in order to be able to take care of myself and others, I needed to keep the lines of communication open with God and my family.

I learned that I needed to listen to my body. There were definitely times when I was just more fatigued than ever before, due to the trauma my body endured. I learned that comparison to other people was an assault on myself. I learned that I needed to be more self-compassionate. I learned that a different experience did not always have to be a better or worse one but could simply be an available alternative. I learned the importance of asking for help. I learned that I could show up authentically, not just as a survivor, but as a thriving woman of God. I learned that I was not just a fighter, but I was a warrior in this thing called life.

I learned that growth never ends if you are open to learning. I learned I could be a successful businesswoman and wife while doing so authentically in the space I created for myself.

The Courage to Stay

Nicol McClendon

"Life adjusts to how you live it."
~ **Nicol McClendon**

The truth is no one is ever fully prepared for what they pray for. We ask God every day to fulfill our wildest dreams, but often, we are ill-prepared for what comes with the fulfillment of those dreams. We make promises about what we will do once God fulfills our dreams, and more promises about what we will not do. Many times, once our dreams are fulfilled, we do not want to work to keep those dreams alive. My mom taught me to be very specific when I pray and to be sure I want what I am praying for, because there are times when we are blessed when we ask God to fulfill a dream, and He does.

I was married to my first husband for 19 years. In the last year of our marriage, I prayed to God for Him to take my husband out of the streets. I asked God to bring him home. I asked God to stop all of the things my husband was doing so that he could be home with our children and me. On the last day of our marriage, my husband came home early. Unusually early. He called and asked what was for dinner. He came home with wood and all the supplies needed to build a doghouse with the kids, something he had talked about doing forever. He and the children worked on the deck for hours building that doghouse. Once their quality time was complete, my husband and I spent our last night of marriage as a loving couple.

The next day, he was killed – murdered in the same streets I had prayed for him to be taken out of. And suddenly, everything I had hoped would eventually happen never would. Suddenly, my life shattered into pieces. I was devastated. I was not prepared. I felt my prayer was fulfilled, but that I had not been as specific as I should have been. For years I carried the guilt that my unspecific prayers caused the death of my husband. I did not question God. I accepted that my husband was forever out of the streets, and home in our hearts forever.

During the eight years following my husband's passing, I prayed to God every day. I prayed not only to be free from the pain of loss and the emptiness I felt, but also to receive the opportunity to do all the things my husband and I had once talked about doing: traveling, starting a business, and providing a good life for our children.

I had been a writer growing up. In high school, I spent most of my days writing short stories and poems. My dream was to be a great orator, standing on stages, giving speeches, and wowing the masses with my creative imagination. And so, a part of my grieving process was to journal. I wrote short stories about my life. Poems about the love I had lost, and the love I wanted – stories about traveling the world. Eventually, I started traveling. I traveled with my children. I joined a travel group, and also traveled with people I met locally who enjoyed traveling. I felt free every time the wheels went up. I loved flying. I loved visiting different countries. One day on a 14- hour trip from Dubai with my daughter, I conceived of my first business. I decided I would be an independent travel agent helping women and families. My business would focus on providing affordable luxury travel.

I also began writing more. . . a lot more. I noticed the more I wrote, the better I felt. Writing was therapy. I decided I would tell my story, and in telling my story, I created my second business as an author. I dubbed myself "The Authorprenuer with a Passion for Travel." By the time the flight had landed, I was several chapters into my first book, and my travel business had a name. I stepped off the plane with a plan and went to work immediately. I would write every day, and I would have early morning meetings with contacts I acquired from my travels. I was also a mother and had a full-time job that I needed to pay the bills and keep a roof over our heads. I was also a single woman, and this was a new and different experience for me.

The joy I felt when writing reawakened me, and I found that traveling was also great therapy. Traveling opened me up to a whole world of opportunity and enabled meeting new people. It also helped to pass the time. While traveling and writing, I prayed often and long. I prayed for my businesses to be successful, for my children to heal through the process of adapting to their new normal of life after the loss of their father. And I was praying for a man – not just any man, but a husband.

While I was praying, I was working. I was working on me, becoming a better woman and mother. And I was working on my businesses. I officially became a businesswoman when I published my first book, and I felt amazing. I also started booking trips and earning a commission as a travel agent. My children were coping. My prayers were being answered, and I continued to work and pray. But I was still praying for an extraordinary love. I wanted a man who was emotionally available, kind, caring, generous, and one who loved me more than anything or anyone else. Then one day, I met him, and he was just about everything I had prayed for. We fell in love almost instantly. It turned out he was praying to God for me while I was praying for him!

Over the course of the next year, we did everything I dreamed of and everything I asked God to give me. We traveled together. He would listen to and learn with me when I took my travel agent courses. He would read the questions on my test, and I would answer while I was writing or being a mother. We danced. We went on couples' outings. He was a role model in the community, well respected and loved, tall (lol), and he wanted to be my husband. Within one year of dating, we were engaged, and soon after, we celebrated by becoming partners in life and love.

Ten short days after our celebration of love, he was diagnosed with a potentially terminal illness and needed to begin treatment immediately. And again, my life abruptly changed. I feared losing all the wonderful things this new marriage promised. As my love began treatment to fight his illness, I was right by his side. However, I started to lose sight of my daily responsibilities, including those associated with my businesses. I felt like I was suffocating. I was afraid to die and afraid to live. I wanted to give up, but I had to get up every day. I had children depending on me. My partner was depending on me.

Most people do not understand that grieving is not just losing someone in death. We also grieve the loss of many things, including loss of friendships, loss of finances, and loss of dreams. I was afraid, and I started to grieve the potential loss of a new love. Once you have been through a traumatic experience, those memories live with you forever. At the first familiar sign of grief or trauma, your body, your mind, your complete being begins to go into survival mode. You have to decide at that moment if you are willing to fight through that situation or flee from it.

I convinced myself that I needed to flee. My rationalization was that there was no history there. My self-preservation was to remove myself from the entire situation, and everyone close to it. I shut down. I stopped going to the places that were familiar to US. I limited or ended communication with anyone familiar with US. Also, I stopped writing and dissolved my LLC. The travel business was no more, and I was no longer "The Authorprenuer with a Passion for Travel."

Because of my husband's illness and treatment, we were unable to travel, and writing no longer provided the therapy it once had. I was running away from a situation that made me feel like I had felt eight years prior. I was in survival mode to protect myself. Although I had been known as a fighter, I allowed fleeing this situation to become my coping mechanism. That's when the guilt set in. Here I was feeling sorry for myself and giving up on my dreams. Giving up and not working on the dreams that God had fulfilled. My passion, my gift of writing, I just threw away. My love of traveling and helping others simply dissolved.

Someone I loved was fighting for his life. He was facing the most difficult battle he would ever face, and here I was, feeling sorry for myself. Why? Because I had finally gotten all I thought I deserved? Because he was messing it all up? Yes. So, I wanted to run. No, I did not want to stand and fight. Not this time. Because I had paid my dues and it just was not fair. I believed "paying my dues" before was about building me up to be strong again, but God had answered my prayers. God fulfilled my dreams, but I needed to do the work. See, some want the great marriage, and a successful, lucrative business; however, most do not or will not do the work.

Having been married before, I knew what came with marriage. We stand in front of God and our families, and we say, "for better or for worse." However, we never think the "for worse" will come before the "for better," and most run at the first sign of difficulty. I also knew that a couple either grows together and supports each other, or they grow apart.

Being a smart businesswoman means checking and adjusting often, and as needed. We must practice patience, as with any investment, it takes time and hard work for a business to mature before you see profits. We also need to know when the risk of loss is so great that we need to cut ties. Most businesses have more than one employee or partner that can continue day-to-day operations for the business to thrive; however, I was the most important and only worker. I was the President, Owner, and CEO. But my life partner needed me. I knew that my businesses demanded a lot of my time. . . time I did not have to give, so they would have to wait.

It became increasingly difficult for me to pray. I was afraid to. When I made the initial decision to flee instead of fight and in the process of pulling away from anything familiar to my current situation, I had lost some strong support that I knew I needed to get through this next chapter of life. I needed to be honest with myself about my feelings and reasons for fleeing, for I was now slowly pulling away from my familiar life and my partner.

The first person I opened up to about my feelings to flee was my mom, my biggest supporter and strongest prayer warrior. She said, "Even when you do not pray, God hears your thoughts." She continued and ended with "this is temporary." At that moment, I remembered something I had repeatedly said to myself for encouragement years before during that first tragedy in my life: "If what you are seeing is not what you saw, then what you are seeing is temporary."

The second and most important person I was honest with was my partner in life and love. I was honest, even at the risk of hurting him. We discussed the dreams I felt I had lost, and he expressed his own feelings of guilt for the situation we now faced, for he knew my dreams and expectations going into our partnership. He was honest and acknowledged he felt me slowly pulling away. He shared his fear of losing the dream he had prayed for. He feared losing me. He did not say he feared death; he said he was afraid of losing me. So, I decided to fight. Together we started the journey of his treatment and subsequent recovery. He battled with everything he had with me by his side. When he was weak and had no more of his own to give, I provided every bit of strength he needed. Although it was a very trying year with some wins and many losses, we made it through.

One day, during a hospital visit, I decided to write a Facebook post about resilience. It was prompted by reading many posts and hearing of so many women going through tough times. I simply said, "think about what would happen if you didn't give up. Hold on because I'm holding on with you, and you better not give up." That night, as I was leaving the hospital, a woman reached out to me. She said she had been following me for some time and had read my first book. She asked how I was able to release the story without reliving the pain, and she asked how I felt after it was released. I told her writing my story, and sharing a piece of myself was therapy, and with the writing complete and my story released, I was unburdened, emptied, and able to move on.

Although it was therapeutic for me, for a while, after letting it go, I was lost. I struggled with where to go next. Thinking bigger than just my little book was tough. It was not until I realized the blessing in being empty that everything came full circle. I told her I wanted to tell another story. I just needed someone to allow me to. Someone needed their own release, and I was here when they needed me. However, in the midst of waiting for someone else to tell me their story, chapters of my story were still being written.

She released her story to me that day because she needed to be free. It was killing her, holding it inside. I knew as she poured her story into me, it was therapy for her. I listened intensely, never interrupting because this was my business, and every smart businesswoman knows when to shut up and listen. She finished and was silent for a moment. I asked her how she felt, and she said, "I was so happy to have read your story, but I thought I could never tell the world mine." She said, "you are brave."

As we ended our call, she asked, "Nicol, maybe one day you could tell my story?" "Yes," I simply replied. "Yes."

The Gift of Acceptance

Tangie R. McDougald

"Do the best you can until you know better.
Then when you know better, do better."
~ Maya Angelou

Love don't hurt! Love don't hurt! Love don't hurt! Looking at my reflection in the mirror, I chanted these words over and over again. Then, shaking my head, "Enough! Enough!"

From the pit of my stomach, an unrecognized voice belted out loud. There I stood holding my face. Looking in the mirror. A stranger looked back at me. Her mouth trembled and shook uncontrollably. She touched her cheeks, wiping her teardrops away. She touched her hair and slowly moved her hand across her face, touching the numbness of her lips.

A soft voice muttered, "What happened? What happened? What happened to me?" She repeated this phrase as she slid down the wall. She whispered the Lord's Prayer...

"Our Father which art in heaven, Hallowed be thy name. Thy Kingdom come, Thy will be done in earth, as it is in heaven. Give us this day our daily bread. And forgive us our debts, as we forgive our debtors. And lead us not into temptation but deliver us from evil; For thine is the kingdom, and the power, and the glory, for ever. Amen."

-Matthew 6:9-13

What seemed like hours later, I finally rose from a fetal position off of the cold, tiled floor. There I stood looking into the same mirror. This time I stared with confidence. There was no trembling, no tears, and no numbness. I yelled, "Fuck him! Fuck him! Fuck him! I deserve better than this shit!" It was at that moment, I knew it was time to end my marriage.

Over the years, we cultivated what I thought were special alliances among friends. They frequented our home and spent major holidays with us. Often, we confided with one another with the intention to foster stronger unions. That all changed once the ink was dry on the divorce papers.

Soon after my divorce was final, I ran into one of the couples at a clothing store. I made eye contact with the wife, but she quickly turned down an aisle. I eventually caught up with the couple, but before I could speak, the husband, with a smirk of disgust on his face, stated, "So I heard your divorce is final." He added, "We don't believe in divorce, regardless of the reasons behind it." He proceeded to walk away. His wife stood there in discomfort. He yelled across the store, "I'm ready to go!" That was her cue. Her last words to me were, "Girl, I'm gonna call you." Needless to say, I have never seen or heard from them again. This is one example of many friendships that ended once my divorce became final. I quickly learned, not everyone will cheer for you at your party. Not everyone will celebrate or support your life changes.

The feeling of rejection hit hard when it came to my family. Prior to my divorce, I would go to my mother and try to consult with her about my marital problems. She would highlight his good qualities. She said things like, "He helps you with the kids. He cooks and he cleans. He takes good care of you." I tried verbalizing my pain with my dad, but he would brush me off. Minimizing my situation, he would say, "I don't get involved in people relationships. That's your husband. You have to figure it out." Figure it out?

Being turned away by my parents hardened me. The feeling of being rejected throbbed like an infected wound spreading across my body. I am the youngest girl in my family. Child number five out of six children. I was the first to purchase a home and the first to marry. I am the big, little sister who always showed up and fixed problems among us. So, the notion that my parents would not support me through my divorce never crossed my mind. I had to accept that this was my journey, and during this stretch in my life, I was riding it alone.

Eventually, I walked away from my marriage. I took all my clothing. Except for my wedding gown. That wedding gown, so symbolic of our relationship, I intentionally left behind. I placed it in the middle of the cold, dark basement, hanging from the ceiling. Snapping my fingers, singing, and dancing, "But your lies ain't working now. Look who's hurting now. See I had to shut you down. I had to shut you down." As I pursued my freedom from the bondage of my bad marriage, this song became my anthem. I started my mornings jamming to "Heard It All Before" by Sunshine Anderson.

I stared in the mirror, standing on the tips of my toes. I turned my body from one side to the other, with one hand on my hip and the other on my stomach. "Yes," I said, "Yes!" As I shook my head in acknowledgment of my curvaceous figure. I was 60 pounds lighter, feeling Tony The Tiger, GRRR-EAT! The anticipation of becoming a 32-year-old single mother of three couldn't have felt more divine.

It was July 22, 2003, the day after my daughter's 6th birthday. I took a deep breath and walked down the courthouse steps as a single woman. All the bad memories of my marriage flashed before me. I counted as I walked down each step:

1-no longer will I be physically abused.
2-no longer will I be verbally abused.
3-no longer will I be financially abused.
4-no longer will I neglect myself.
5-no longer will I be a victim.

Each step I took, my body felt lighter and lighter. The 60 pounds of weight I lost were burdens left on those courthouse steps. The warmth of the sun gleamed on my face as I put my vintage Versace sunglasses on and clutched my Fendi bag. I walked away with the dissolution of marriage papers in my hand. I was determined never to look back.

NEW BEGINNINGS

> "Father God, my redeemer, I pray that the next man is sent by you. I pray he is the opposite of my ex-husband. I pray for a God-fearing man. A man who treats me like a queen. A man who loves his family. A man who is faithful and trustworthy. A man who is a protector and a provider. In Jesus' name, I pray. Amen"

I never believed in fairytales, because nothing came easy in my life, but I prayed for my fairytale wish, anyway. A few weeks before Thanksgiving, I decided to go to Mohegan Sun Casino. This was the first night I met Kyle. He came on pretty strong; he flirted relentlessly. I was flattered by the attention, but I wasn't looking to find a man.

Kyle had different plans. That night he called his mother. He talked with excitement, "I just met my wife! We're going to get married in Vegas!" As he passed the phone to me, he said to his mother, "Say hi to my wife." My thoughts were, this man has had too much to drink, and he has clearly lost his mind. As the night went on, I began to play along. It was something about his attention, effort, and consistency that attracted me.

We began dating and became a couple quickly. We talked a lot about our future and the goals that we both wanted to accomplish. We agreed that I would enroll in school. In addition, we would open a clothing and a convenience store. Finally, I felt like I had someone who wanted to see me live my best life.

We were seven years into our relationship when we received a visit from our pastor. The pastor inquired about our intentions for our relationship. He asked, "Are you planning to get married?" "No," I explained, "I have been married before, and I'm not ready for marriage again. I know I have a man that loves me. He showers me with gifts. He opens doors, pull chairs from the table, and he kisses my hands. I am his "sugarfoot" and he has no problem proclaiming it to the world." I went on to say Kyle had asked me to marry him several times throughout our relationship, but I felt like what we had was working for us. You know that saying, 'if it ain't broke, don't fix it?' I asked.

Kyle spoke up and softly stated, "I am willing to marry her, but we are good either way." The pastor ended the visit in prayer.

As time went on, we continued to work hard. I was still pursuing my education and we traveled a lot. I should have been happy, but I began to feel a void. I would wake up to use the bathroom and find Kyle soaking in the tub, talking to God. The bathroom became his prayer room. Kyle no longer slept in the bed. He would have the jacuzzi on, candles lit, his Bible, and the *Daily Bread*. Oftentimes, he would submerge himself underwater. As he rose his head from underneath, he rose up worshipping.

Kyle would fall asleep in the tub. I would wake him afraid he was going to drown. He would refuse to get out of the water and would welcome me to join him. I would decline.

The bathroom is located behind our bedroom wall. So, I

would overhear him praising God. I grew irritated when he worshiped. I started closing our bedroom door and turning on the television in an attempt to drown out his voice. Kyle tried grasping any moments he could to share the Word with me.

Anytime I would go to use the bathroom, he would start talking about God or reading Scripture. "Tangie," he would begin, "This is coming from the Book of Psalms," or "Tangie, listen to today's Word coming from the *Daily Bread*." Kyle was excited about God and wanted to pour onto me. At one point, I began turning off the bathroom light so that I could use the bathroom in peace, but this would only encourage him to become louder. If he couldn't read God's gospel, then he would sing or pray.

One day, I was awakened by Kyle's prayer to God. His voice was pronounced and forceful as he prayed: "Father, you said, 'ask and it shall be done.' Father, I pray in petition that you give peace to Tangie." Instantly, I sat up in my bed. I listened to Kyle cry out to the Lord. Tears flowed down my face. My soul ached as I wept. I was full of emotions, confused, angry, and scared. Worshipping wasn't new to me. As I was raised in a small Pentecostal church, but this was different. It was at that moment that I recognized that Kyle was engaged in spiritual warfare, fighting to save my soul and our relationship. That night I wept, repented, and surrendered to God.

After that night, I became more receptive and reflective. I would wake up in tears. There was no reason why I cried. I would be in deep thought. I began to talk to God. Evaluating my life, I would take advantage of these nights. I would meditate and search for understanding. I asked myself, "Am I not in peace? Am

I not happy?" Through my life reflections, I discovered I was angry. I was angry about my relationships. I was mad at my ex-husband for not loving me. I was mad at my parents for not being there for me. I was mad at Kyle for showing me love.

The internal feeling of rejection I had didn't start in the midst of my troubled marriage. This feeling initiated in my youth, and it carried over into my adulthood. I discovered, no one had taught me how to love. I idealized an image of what love and relationships were supposed to look like from shows like "The Cosby Show" and "The Fresh Prince of Bel-Air," but my relationships never mirrored those shows. Instead, I actually identified with shows like "Sally Jessy Raphael" and "The Geraldo Rivera Show." The dysfunctional dynamics in relationships they displayed resonated as normalcy in my world.

In 1999, BET's show "Teen Summit" aired a campaign to end domestic violence. They broke down what unhealthy relationships look like. Then, they specified how to identify if you were in an abusive relationship. I sat in awe. I had mixed emotions. I was shocked that my relationship consisted of every red flag they provided. I was happy to find out I was not alone. I was scared because I knew I had to make this stop. I guess my dad was right, "I had to figure it out."

IN MY PURSUIT OF HAPPINESS

Our desire to open our businesses came into fruition. Some of the obstacles we faced in our businesses were that our approaches and views were different. Kyle knew a lot of people. He had street connections, and his business strategies were influenced by this. I took a more conservative route in my approach to business. Some people would say it was the best of both worlds. We could utilize our platforms together to become successful. However, it created conflict between us. I didn't like the direction Kyle preferred, and I didn't like the way he operated as a business owner. I wanted to do things my way. There was no room for compromise. Eventually, we decided to close both businesses.

During this time, I was applying for graduate school. While going through the application process, I was instructed to write an essay regarding my future goals. This led me to my original questions in examining myself: What is peace? What is happiness?

Throughout my life, I've been told God has given us all special gifts and talents so we can live life fully for him. As I thought about my life experiences, I noticed a pattern. My life was defined by what I had been through. I lived my life feeling unworthy. I was unworthy to be loved, I thought. This became my belief system. This was my lie. This lie crippled my ability to find peace and happiness because it suppressed my truth.

My truth was this: my parents had always loved me. Their love extended from what they knew as love. From my mother's view, love meant holding onto her family, finding the positives in her relationship, and safeguarding those by any means necessary. My dad displayed his love by respecting and empowering me to make my own decisions, even if they were mistakes. He taught me how to clean up my own mess.

This epiphany was deep. It all made sense now. I thought, I

have not been at peace. My soul has been smothered through years of heartache and pain. My past experiences hindered my ability to be happy. And it was hell. I realized I was living in hell. I thought, what was the purpose of getting a divorce if I was not going to live in peace and happiness? The more I processed, the better I understood how my past relationship was still affecting me.

My ex-husband's voice played back in my head, "Nobody gon' love your ass!" Hmph, I thought. He was right, and he was winning! These experiences hardened me. My heart was cold and dark, like the basement where I left my wedding gown. No one was going to love me, not because I wasn't worthy, but because I wouldn't truly allow them to love me. I realized I was afraid of love.

It was at that moment that I understood I had wasted nine years in my current relationship. Nine years I had been ducking and dodging love. Nine years post-divorce, and I was still held in bondage by a toxic relationship. I was disgusted that I wasted so much time self-sabotaging my life.

FREE AT LAST

Through my examination of self, I decided to no longer live in my lie. I vowed to no longer hold onto negative thoughts and feelings of unworthiness and rejection. I had decided to accept my parents for who they were. I accepted their disposition of love. I no longer held onto being angry. Once my anger was released, I was able to work on my acceptance of self. I explored things that made me happy, and things that made me feel complete.

Eliminating these negative views allowed me to begin to heal my soul. Life was evolving in front of me. My body shifted from feelings of coldness and darkness. You could hear the rusted shackles being released from my ankles. As I rose to stand up, the sun became brighter and brighter. The grass smelled fresh, and the yard was full of beautiful flowers. There wasn't a cloud in the sky. I looked to the right, and there was a rainbow in a perfect horizon. There I stood, standing in peace.

Being at peace allowed me to grow spiritually. I noticed God had been answering my prayers all the while. God had sent me my husband, but I was too angry to see. He sent a God-fearing man, but I was too angry to hear. All the qualities of a man I prayed for were with me all along. I had to forgive and accept the transgressions that I've encountered in my life.

My perception of our relationship had changed. I grew eager and excited about life. I was ready for a commitment. I was ready to marry. I would say things like, "Oh, I'm not being with no one for ten years without marriage. When are we getting married? Do you want a small wedding or big wedding?" I was excited about the notion of being his wife. That came with a different kind of nagging. Kyle would humbly reply, "Whenever, whatever, and however, you want it." We invited the same pastor over that we turned away three years before. He once again prayed over us and gave his blessing in marriage.

In August 2014, we flew to Hawaii and got married. Eloping was the best expression of freedom that I could give myself. I was in love, and I was happy. Now that I had found love, I vowed never to let it go. Kyle continued to support me in pursuing what I loved. This time it felt different.

We lost two businesses because I didn't feel worthy of having them. I gave up and rejected them because I didn't know how to pour love into them. This time I was ready to pour love into my business. I was able to accept the differences in our business styles. I looked for his opinion and made concessions, whereas before I would shut his ideas down. I recall looking at property and signing the lease to my office before I became licensed by the State. Unemployed and unbothered, I then handed in my resignation and spent a few weeks vacationing in Florida.

The day after I returned from vacation, I walked into my new office. I checked my voicemail, and I had three messages. Two were from old clients that had decided to follow my practice, and one was a new client. I checked my email and found notification that I was fully licensed. As I sat there in disbelief, all I could do was praise God. I had thought if I could establish at least ten clients weekly, I would be able to manage financially. I started working on obtaining approval with insurance companies and before I was ready to open for business, I had a full caseload. There was no advertising or marketing done to obtain clients.

This was all God.

THE GLOW UP

I attribute my success in business to God. I was able to see Kyle as a vessel that had been sent by God. Once I submitted to loving myself, I was able to become free and love life. Through my own healing, I've found, you can't find your purpose without finding your happiness. You can't find your happiness if you don't accept love in your life. I've learned to love.

There I stood looking into the mirror on the tips of my toes. I turned my body from one side to the other. With one hand on my hip and the other on my stomach. This time I smiled. I love the glow that shined back at me. A glow of peace. Peace within myself. Peace within my marriage. Peace within my business.

"Thank you, Jesus! Thank you, Jesus! Thank you, Jesus!" I chanted over and over again, looking at my reflection in the mirror. Shaking my head, I shouted, "Hallelujah! Hallelujah!" Hands lifted in the air, singing, and praising, "He saw the best in me. When everyone else around me could only see the worst in me."

Does anybody have their testimony? When folks wrote you off. Said you would never make it. What did He see? He saw the best in me." This song became my new anthem. I start my mornings praising God as I worship to music by Marvin Sapp.

The testimony I share today comes from a lifetime of tests that I had to endure. I am thankful for the richness I've learned to accept. . .richness in my mind, body, and soul.

Test and Trials of a Blended Family

Cherry L. Jackson

"I can do all things
through Christ who strengthens me."
~ **Philippians 4:13**

When I got married, I married into a blended family. And it challenged me. Being called into ministry, I was ministering to others, yet I was unable to minister to my blended family, and this caused me a great amount of turmoil. How was it that I was ministering to others about love and forgiveness, yet struggling to walk in it for myself?

I would come home from a high time at church, and then we would get a phone call or text that would just ruin my day, and sometimes my whole week. I kept praying, Lord, how do I get past this? I knew the answer, but I didn't want to do it; I had to pray for them. . . The Bible says to pray for your enemies. The Lord showed me a dream, and in that dream, I was praying for one of the other mothers in my blended family on the phone, and she was in tears. I woke up and just laughed. I said, Lord, we don't even talk, so that dream is not going to come true! I thought it was silly, but it truly makes sense to me now.

I met my husband over 18 years ago at a movie theater. What I found odd on that particular day was there was no woman with him, but he did have a group of little girls, all under the age of five. I thought, What a handsome guy! Where is his wife, and who do all these little girls belong to? I assumed a few had to belong to him because what man, in his right mind, would take out a group of small girls unless he had one or two of his own among them? Once the movie was over, and we were all exiting the theater, one of the little girls had an untied shoelace, and my BFF, Darniece, kindly bent down and tied it for her. In the lobby, he began to express his gratitude for the kind gesture as we all chatted briefly.

He told me his name was Richard Jackson. He instructed the girls to hold hands in a line, and to my surprise, serendipitously, the younger of the twins grabbed my hand and wouldn't let go. So, I ended up walking with them to their car, which, to my shock and surprise, was a taxicab! Oh no! After putting the little girl in the taxi, the tall, dark, and handsome guy asked for my phone number. Was he kidding? With all of those kids! I didn't think so! My first thought was to give him the wrong number. But, he was so handsome and seemed so nice, and I couldn't resist. After all, we could become just "good friends," you know what I mean?

When Darniece and I got in the car, she gave me the business. "Did you give him the right number? Was he really driving a taxicab? And did all five of the girls belong to him?" We both just laughed about it and went home.

Well, the phone rang around 8:30 pm that night, and it was Richard. Within the first five minutes of our phone conversation,

I had to know. So, I asked him straight up who all those children belonged to. Surely all five couldn't belong to him! Whew... I found out three of the five little girls were his. Big relief, right? And then he mentioned he had two other children. . .a boy, and another girl! With that being said, I knew this was going nowhere fast, and decided a "good friend" he would be.

Who dreams of marrying someone with one ex-wife, two other mothers, and a total of five children? I don't think anyone does, and this surely wasn't going to be my story. I had already been married and divorced, but didn't have children. In fact, I was told by medical experts that it would be almost impossible for me to conceive. My former husband and I had even attempted artificial insemination, a very uncomfortable and expensive procedure. Unfortunately, there was no success.

Richard and I wed three years after meeting, in July 2005. My body soon started to feel funny, but surely, I wasn't pregnant because the doctors had said it would be a slim chance. I took about five pregnancy tests, and they all read positive! But I didn't believe the tests because they came from Family Dollar and they were the cheap brand. So, I finally went to my doctor, who confirmed that I was actually pregnant, and my child would be here on February 14, 2006. What a Valentine's gift that would be!

You can't always trust the doctor's word, but in this case, she was right. Now, there were a total of six children. Three girls – a set of twins and a younger sister by his ex-wife – his oldest daughter from his teenaged interest, another son who just kinda happened, and our child. We laugh about it now, but I would tease him and say, "Papa was a rolling stone."

At the time we married, most people didn't really discuss blended families, or 'bonus' children, and 'bonus' moms or dads. When two people decided to get married, they did just that, and no one really considered the children or other families that would be affected and included.

Now, if you think I didn't have major concerns about Richard and his whole package, I did, but one part of me wanted to think that all involved would be mature adults, and we would live happily ever after. Boy, was I wrong! It was far more difficult than I had ever imagined. In fact, I am still healing from some of the hurts and wounds that I received in that blended family relationship. I would love to say I was the perfect bonus mom, but unfortunately, I was not. However, going into that situation, I was open-minded and thought everyone else would be too. I quickly realized that wasn't going to be the case, and my world was about to be turned upside down and inside out.

One incident I vividly remember was planning to take all the kids to Disney World. This was a great idea, right? I thought so. This would be an icebreaker for everyone, because everyone loves Disney. I was so sure that the mothers would think this was a great idea for me and their kids to bond, and no doubt the kids would be ecstatic. OMG! I had never in my life fought so hard to plan a vacation! Why was this so difficult? We received every excuse in the book on why the trip couldn't happen, but none of it made sense. We were talking Disney, so what was the problem?

There were several excuses given on why the children couldn't go, such as the dates that were provided weren't going to work, so I switched the dates. Then, all of a sudden, the children got sick two weeks prior before the departure date was set, so we were told they wouldn't be able to attend, wait.. what? So, I eventually called the doctor's office to get the diagnoses, only to be informed the children were cleared to travel, and it was not a big deal. We were even told that one child just wasn't interested in going. Here again, we are talking Disney, and what child under the age of ten is not interested in going to Disney? What was this really about? Was it about Disney, or was it something deeper?

After 15 years of being enmeshed with a blended family, I can share the good, bad, and the OH so ugly. For the first several years, I was trying to figure this "blended" stuff out. I instantly went from being single to married with five children. Unfortunately, I didn't have a 'how-to' or 'quick fix' book. Now let me remind you again there were three mothers involved here, and that wasn't going to make this blend easy. In fact, everything seemed complicated, and I felt like family and situations pushed every button I had, so I found myself quickly getting very frustrated, irritated, cold, and most definitely overwhelmed.

I started to think, this blend is not going to work! It's just too much! So, I eventually started to pull back from the children, my husband, and of course, the other mothers. This had affected me more than I had realized. I was mentally tired, drained, offended, and suffered through several sleepless nights. At several points, I even found myself wanting to file for divorce.

I felt like my world had come to an end, and everything was spiraling out of control. I had allowed the life and energy to be sucked right out of me. Everything turned into a fight with the other mothers. I would say blue, one would say black, and another would say green. No one ever wanted to agree, even on the simplest things. Why did everything have to be so complicated? I truly didn't understand it.

I remember buying the children's clothes, and one mother sent them all back in trash bags. WHY? I remember going to go pick up the children, and no one would answer the door, when clearly, they were inside. WHY? I should have realized you must accept people where they are in life, mentally, physically, spiritually, and financially, because if they're not in a good state of mind and unhappy, they will make things very complicated in a blended relationship. However, I eventually found myself in a dark place, mentally and spiritually. I had become silently angry and bitter, but who would know or see it because when we went out in public, I had to put on the 'happy blended family' face, even when I was feeling miserable and torn up on the inside.

All the bickering, arguing, yelling, screaming matches, threats, court appearances, silent treatment, and verbal attacks had taken a toll on me. Or rather, I had allowed these things to affect me, and to be honest, I really didn't know how to handle this blended situation effectively. So, I became distant to all parties involved, including the children. Looking back now, I should have reached out for help through counseling, but me, 'Ms. know everything,' did not.

Sometimes, you don't know how something has affected you until you come out of it. I was a mess mentally, but I looked good on the outside. Life had beaten me down to where some days I didn't want to get out of bed. I had lost my zeal for life and was just existing. I had fallen into a slight depression and didn't even realize it. I had put this wall up, and I was on guard, always ready for the next attack; because I knew one was coming.

Looking back, if I had to do it all over again, things would be totally different. For starters, I would not entertain any unnecessary or foolish conversations. For example, telling me what kind of car I should drive is a pointless conversation. Why should I have a conversation about the car that I'm driving, especially if I'm paying the bill? It's a waste of time and energy, and definitely not productive. I would love despite any conflict, displaying love and maturity at all times – or I would try. This doesn't mean I'd allow someone to take advantage of me.

How do you love someone who keeps cursing you out, or intentionally tries to bring harm and confusion to your family? It truly takes the love of God! It's not easy, but there are solutions. One solution is to cease all conversation – just hang up and block them – and pray that one day you can have a reasonable and respectful conversation. Until then, blocking is amazing! I should have let my husband handle most of the issues, but when I felt they were trying to manipulate him and trying to take advantage, I felt I had to step in. My husband would tell me many times to let it go, saying it was not that big of a deal. But me being who I am, I couldn't sit back and let it go at that time. I probably caused myself many migraine headaches and sleepless nights.

If you are over the age of 40 and marry someone, more than likely, you will experience a blended family relationship. I understand blended families should be considered case by case situation – solutions are not one size fits all. However, I have a few things I can share if you want to become better and not bitter in a blended family. A truly meaningful and honest conversation must take place, first between the marrying couple, to make sure this is really what you want to do, and it will be a good fit for all involved. In this conversation, you should discuss any potential issues that you think may cause a problem in your relationship down the road.

An open discussion about your relationship with the ex, and related challenges, along with any mental illness challenges, and any known bad or violent behaviors, is part of this. Don't be afraid to ask difficult questions. Will there be religious conflicts? Do you pay child support, and will this affect the family finances? Is another ethnicity involved? How different are the cultures? Will your grocery list change? Yes, I said grocery list! You may be told one day, "I don't eat that food anymore." This all may seem funny and trivial, but you will thank me later. I'm not talking about something that I heard about, I'm speaking on things that I have personally dealt with in my own house. I would strongly advise counseling sessions with a professional, as well. Lay down a foundation on what to expect from everyone. This includes children and the ex, because no one has the extra time or energy to deal with unnecessary foolishness.

There first must be mutual respect from all involved; you may not like me, and I might not like you, but a level of respect and civil behavior must exist. Having a parenting plan and child support agreement in place may make life easier, as well. If you don't need it, great! But from my experience, I can tell you that marriage, or getting involved with someone else changes things. If you see issues starting to arise concerning visitation or child support, do yourself a favor, just go to court and get legal documentation in place. This will save you from a headache down the road.

You would hope that everyone would be mature and amicable

when blending, but unfortunately, many won't be. That's when attorneys come into play, and they wind up making significant money off individuals who aren't reasonable or mature enough to put a plan in place themselves. (So, you mean to tell me that someone would rather pay an attorney minimally $1500, just to put a visitation and support agreement in place?) Unfortunately, we had to take each mother to court just to be able to see the children. For the life of me, I don't see why two adults can't sit down and reasonably discuss a parenting plan and finances that they would need to adequately take care of a child, without having to pay an attorney or a judge to make that decision.

It truly blows my mind, and it just doesn't make good sense to me! However, I do understand that sometimes it's necessary to get an attorney involved just to control chaos and confusion. In many cases, the foundation is not laid overnight, so it can be a process that takes months, if not years, to settle. Most have to make adjustments to smooth out the kinks when blending.

Manipulation can come in many forms. Adults and children may try to play one against the other. I've heard so many stories, and I definitely have my own about children being manipulated, and even brainwashed by one parent. Some of the awful things that may be said to an innocent child include: he or she doesn't love you anymore; they have moved on with their new family; they don't financially support you; they didn't want to attend your event at school; you can't visit, because they don't want you at their home; they treat their child better than you, so stay away.

How are children supposed to handle that or know what is true and what is a lie? Unfortunately, they don't, and you can't control what another parent may say or tell the child. All you can do is talk to your children truthfully and kindly when the opportunity arises, tell them they are loved and pray that the Lord will open up their understanding.

Please understand that children can be manipulative as well; however, I would expect the parent to recognize the behavior and deal with it accordingly. When children are part of your relationship dynamic, then who you marry or date, and what happens in your house, or her house, or his house, absolutely matters. I believe I have a responsibility to know the background of the individual my child is going to be around, so it's very much my business!

And, finally, the most important factors in any blended family are LOVE and FORGIVENESS; these are small words with powerful meaning. In 1 Peter 4:8, it says, "Above all things have intense and unfailing love for one another, for love covers a multitude of sins." And in Matthew 18:21-22, "Then Peter came to Jesus and asked, 'Lord, how many times shall I forgive my brother or sister who sins against me? Up to seven times?' Jesus answered, 'I tell you, not seven times, but seventy-seven times.'"

So, what does that really mean for us in a blended family? We must learn to love unconditionally, and constantly forgive even when being lied to, talked about, criticized, not liked, cursed out, plotted against – learn how to love with the love of God. Love wins! Forgive, because we are all going to make mistakes, or say and do hateful things that we will regret later. The quicker you learn how to love and forgive, the better you will be.

To be honest, it took me a while, and I'm still growing. After raising six children, five of which I didn't birth, I will say it has been a life-changing experience, and to be honest, if I had to do it all over again and had to deal with the same individuals, I would not! I would save myself from all the unnecessary stress I encountered. There were many days and nights where I was on my knees, praying and crying out to the Lord. "How do I get past all of this?" I would ask. "Wouldn't it be easier just to walk away from it all?" I would be fine as long as I didn't have to deal with the children's mothers; they had become a stumbling block to me, and also my ministry. Just like in the cartoons, I would see the devil on one shoulder and an angel on the other, each whispering in my ear. Many days I wanted to let those mothers have a piece of my mind, but then that angel would say, "Just pray for them."

I'm sure many are wondering where Rick was in all of this.

He was right there with me, fighting on every hand; some battles he asked me not to fight, but I fought anyway. I was determined not to let anyone get over or take advantage of us. We often talk about how things should have been done differently to make life easier and avoid blended family drama. All of the children are over 18 now, so they are not required to come over anymore.

I would love to tell you that we are all still happily blended, but unfortunately, we are not. With all of the manipulation, bickering, arguing, and trying to make sure the truth was told, things just didn't go as planned. We are not blended and happy as I hoped we would be.

* * *

I've learned a few valuable lessons from this blended situation:

- Don't fall into the pitfalls of drama from the other parent. Learn to ignore and only engage when it comes to issues with the children.

- Love the children unconditionally, ignoring what another parent may have said or done in reference to you. You can't stop anyone from putting false allegations on you.

- Prayer is a must!

- Forgive quickly. This will make life better for you. It doesn't mean you have to deal with disrespect of any kind.

- You and your spouse must stand together on all things, not allowing anyone to come between you or disrupt your union. You simply must be on the same page.

Had I followed my own advice 15 years ago, I would be in a much better space today, and it would have saved me from so many emotional scars and heartaches. . .from being offended, mad, angry, bitter, you name it. Remember that love and forgiveness make the difference in you – not the other person. And remember that crazy dream I had? The one where I was praying for one of the mothers on the phone?

Well, six months after I had that dream, it came to pass. IT CAME TRUE! I had to pray for someone who had wished me harm. But now, she was crying, and we were connecting.

My prayer is that every blended family can come to an agreement that works for their household and learn to love with the love of God. How awesome would it be if two blended families could come together and dine at the same table! That didn't happen for me, but maybe it will for you. I would love to sit with the other mothers and get their perspectives. I've always wanted to have a table talk, but Jada beat me to it. I pray that I have said something that has encouraged, inspired, or enlightened you in some way.

God bless!

Out of Chaos into Greatness

Frances Ann Bailey

"Broken Crayons Still Color."
~ **Shelley Hitz**

As a young woman, I always dreamed of having a fairytale, two-parent home, a loving husband, and financial stability. But there were giants that stood ahead of me.

There were many sacrifices and life punches I endured to reach a happy and stable place where I would feel successful in my family life, as well as in my career goals. At the young age of 18, coming from a sanctified Christian family, I had to deliver some heartbreaking news to my parents. I found out I was pregnant with my first child, who would be born out of wedlock, which went totally against my family's beliefs.

The very thought of abortion was out of the question; I did not want to dishonor my own godly principles. My daughter wasn't a mistake. She just wasn't in my plans at that point in my life. But I felt I had let my parents and myself down for not being able to fulfill my fairytale dream.

One of my most difficult sacrifices was turning down my

acceptance into college, which was something I never imagined doing. Different things began to go through my mind trying to seek solutions to make it up to my parents for crushing their hearts. They were my role models; I wanted to be just like them growing up. One of my biggest desires was having a husband and a stable father figure for my child, just as I had growing up. It was important for me to keep the family values that were engraved in my heart, which was the reason I decided to get married.

My future husband would be a guy I met through one of my siblings. He was six years older than I was, so he appeared to be a capable provider, as he would buy things I couldn't afford on my own for my daughter and me. He often did things to make me feel wanted. Frequently, he would make special trips to my home after work to rub my feet, send unexpected loving text messages, and cook for me. He always seemed very protective of me. I believed he was the perfect guy to marry – even though he had hit me while we were dating. I was sure that once I became his wife, he would realize how much I meant to him, and he would change.

After marrying him, it felt good to walk around saying that I was a wife. My father would smile and tell me how much he loved me and to keep following what God's Word says to do. My mother would say, "Baby, if you're happy, then I'm happy." This made me feel so at peace with them; it was a relief from my initial feelings of dishonoring them. I knew that I had pleased my parents, and I didn't want to disappoint them again. But in reality, while I was pleasing my parents, I was drowning in a life of bondage.

Maintaining appearances made this marriage look like the dream I always wanted it to be. No one imagined the life I was experiencing behind closed doors. I spent many days and many years smiling in public, but crying in private, and to be honest, it drained the very soul out of me. My so-called, God-ordained marriage that seemed to be a life of joy was really a life of misery. In that marriage, there wasn't a day that went by that I didn't feel worthless. Experiencing so much verbal, emotional, and physical abuse hurt my body and my spirit. He would slam my head into windows, snatch my earrings out of my ears until my earlobes ripped, and throw me across the living room. I couldn't bathe unless he told me to do so. I would sit as he would just pour 12 pack after 12 pack of beers over me as if I was the dirt on the ground. He would tell me I would never be anything, and I felt like I didn't have any control over anything in that relationship.

This all led me to different paths of life that I wasn't supposed to be on. I began to behave in ways not aligned with my character and cultivated several bad habits. Despite all that I went through, I never left because I feared financial instability. My low self- esteem and lack of confidence led me to question myself. "How would I make it without him?" I thought. He was the breadwinner of the family. I didn't even have to work unless I wanted to, and soon I believed I wasn't capable.

Staying so long in that toxic environment began to stain my life. I had started to turn into somebody that people never knew – someone I didn't know myself. After about two years of marriage, I had totally lost who I was and was doing whatever I had to do to either make sure I could numb the pain, or hide the scars, even if my actions meant losing all moral and ethical standards. I began to self-medicate my empty places by abusing alcohol and pain- killers, and by looking for love in all the wrong places. I couldn't see past my hurt, so nothing else mattered to me. I had come to the lowest point of my life, and I felt everything was beyond repair. Divorce was what I knew I needed. How could I face even more embarrassment from my parents by once again going against their Christian values so publicly?

Protecting my daughter was my one priority, and I knew I was choosing between life and death. So, I made the choice to divorce. However, the day I made up in my mind to go and stay gone was also the day he tried to kill me. As I walked out of the legal aid office after getting my paperwork to help with my divorce, He pulled me into his car and rode me around for hours and hours, beating me inside of his car. He was banging my head up against the car window. He had been drinking that day, and that's all I could smell in the car as it was stuffed up – he kept the windows rolled up so nobody could hear my cry. After begging him to stop hitting me, he then took out a gun, and put it on his lap, and said, "if I can't have you, nobody will."

As he drove me down a dirt lane, he started to put the gun to my head, with tears rolling down his face. At that moment, a car came out of nowhere, which made him put the gun down, and he waved out the car window, signaling for it to go around him. As the other car began to drive around us, I hit the unlock button in the car door and tried to jump out. He grabbed my shirt and began to pull me out of the car on the driver's side. The driver of the other car screamed, "Let her go!" I literally wiggled out of my shirt and began to run with nothing but a bra on. I jumped into her car, and she took off to take me to the hospital. He then attempted to hit her car head-on. I had seen my life flash right before my eyes.

Enduring so much pain, all that abuse, and my self-medicating abuse, I came to the realization that I was no longer going to be just a wife; I deserved to be treated like a queen, and that is what I would be shooting for from that day forward. I knew that I was a diamond in the eyes of the God that loved me so unconditionally, and I had to stop settling if I wanted a better life for my daughter and me. I decided to take my life back and move out of and on from that flesh-eating marriage. I left the marriage and moved back home with my parents. After my divorce, I learned how loneliness felt. This was unexpected. My mind raced with questions and more self-doubt. How could I ever bounce back from such tragic events? Would I ever heal? Why did I have to go through that? I never wanted a failed marriage, and I definitely didn't want to be alone, yet I found myself trying to pick up the pieces of my broken heart. I felt as though God had failed me, so I drifted away from my relationship with Christ.

After dealing with this unhealthy first marriage, I knew exactly what I needed and deserved when it came to love. No more selling myself short. At least, that what's I promised myself. Unfortunately, I didn't keep my own promise. Loneliness lowered my standards, and I gave myself to many relationships that were unhealthy. Then God sent my husband. My new guy was five years younger than I was, very calm and easy going and very accepting of my child. After years of learning what love wasn't, this man gave me the opportunity to experience all I had hoped and believed love was, but I rejected him. I was so full of fear, resentment, and hurt. Too afraid to trust again, I offered only friendship to a guy who really wanted my heart. I felt like I was protecting myself and controlling the relationship by only being friends with benefits. The plan was not to get emotionally attached, so my heart wouldn't be broken again. He agreed and was patient with my process of trying to heal. However, over the course of our friendship, we were surprised with the pregnancy of our son. We decided to make things official and right, so a year after the birth of my son, our friendship blossomed into romance, and later we became one with God in marriage.

Feeling as though God had answered all of my prayers and seen all my tears, I began once more to turn toward God. After so many years of hurt, abuse, and broken promises, feeling God's grace and freedom was something I thought I would never get to experience again. I finally had a loving husband and father figure for my children. What had broken me in the past also fixed my vision, and during the next phase of my life, I wanted to dedicate my time to a ministry of helping other women overcome what I overcame.

I wasn't suffering abuse in this marriage, and everything was going great until my husband and I were hit with a financial storm sometime later in our marriage. This obstacle began to shift my focus. We were pregnant with our daughter, and we had just closed on our brand-new house. In the process of starting a new job, I went to put in my two weeks' notice, and my job told me to just leave, and I didn't have to come back. I was devastated that now I had to be out of work without pay for an extra two weeks.

What were we supposed to do with a mortgage payment coming up? My husband had the strain of pulling extra hours and working late nights to try to make ends meet.

With the extra load of stress, I almost lost my baby. I remember sitting on the toilet wiping and my toilet tissue turning pink and then red. My heart dropped, and I would pray, "Lord, please get us through this." That moment of our marriage was rough as we began to worry more about the bills than anything else. Our bills began to outweigh our paychecks, and the foundation of our marriage was being tested. I started my new job, and months later, we gave birth to our baby girl. It felt as though things had begun to go back to normal. However, before I knew it, we were hit with another financial storm.

We received notification that we owed the IRS. I didn't qualify for pay while on maternity leave, and my husband's hours at his job were cut tremendously. I remember crying out to God, saying, "Lord, no. . . not again! Why us?" I was trying to remind God that He said in His word that He would make me the head and not the tail. My faith at that moment was put on trial with God. I began to feel as though as soon as we took a couple of steps forward, we got knocked ten more steps back. In a state of panic, I again enrolled in school in hopes that if I furthered my education, maybe I would get a raise in my job.

Things became even tighter as I watched the money my husband worked hard for leave his hands like a flowing river. We were borrowing money, running into debt from swiping credit cards, and living paycheck to paycheck. I would feel a rush of butterflies when the food ran low, or we needed gas in the cars to keep going to work. I didn't want to think about the fact that we were about to run out of money.

Having to borrow money from family members to make ends meet wasn't the life I wanted to live; however, I was my husband's helpmate, and as a wife, I felt I had to make sure I met what funds weren't there. With my husband's hours being cut, I then became the breadwinner. Having to carry the majority of the bills wasn't something I wasn't used to doing, and the financial difficulty began to put more strain on our marriage. We started fighting against each other instead of fighting together. Often, we had to remind each other that we vowed to do this thing together, for richer or poorer. This was something that we just had to get through together, so we would go down in prayer, asking God for a breakthrough and strength.

Through all these back-to-back troubles and obstacles, I drew closer to God, and I started to wonder if this was God's way of telling me something else had to be done. Different storms had come to distract me from the vision God had given me after leaving my first marriage. Upon spending time with God, He revealed to me that I was asking Him to provide more wealth, but He had already given me the power to obtain wealth with my hands. That meant I needed to take action and do whatever God was telling me to do! Nevertheless, I allowed fear to overtake me, and I put my vision on the back burner of my plans. I had started to become comfortable in my discomfort.

Determined to not step outside of my comfort zone, my stress level increased day by day. I was now a student alongside being a wife and a mother. During this period of overwhelming financial strain and multiple responsibilities, my body started to change and fail. There would be days and weeks at a time I would have to call out of work because I couldn't walk or even move my arms. My doctor gave me news that felt like a punch in the face. "You need to file for disability as your condition is now progressing, Mrs. Bailey." He added, "Your co-pay for your medicine is $4,000." We were already in a financial crisis. Being diagnosed with hidradenitis suppurativa, an incurable, chronic, skin condition that limited my mobility, sent chills through me. I remember grabbing my head, clenching my hair and screaming, "This is too much for me! I can't handle this!"

A great fear came over me that I wouldn't be able to help provide for my family as I imagined. Taking weeks off at a time could potentially cause me to lose my job, and how was I even going to afford my medicine?

As awful as those fears were, it was even more hurtful that I had to watch my children's faces of sadness as I struggled to walk or move. My youngest child would look at me with tears in her eyes and say "ouch" because that's all she ever heard me murmur. It crushed my heart every morning watching my oldest child get her little brother and sister ready for me because my pain was so unbearable that I had trouble even getting out of bed.

They saw me day after day in pain, but I wasn't going to let them see me give up. I was determined to embrace the truth that everything I needed was inside of me. I shouldn't have to walk around, living in fear of finances breaking up my marriage or losing my job when my vision of helping others to overcome life obstacles was my calling. I dropped to my knees in prayer, and I asked God to help me to focus, to walk out of my fear, and to give me strength to persevere through my chronic condition to reach my destiny.

I knew I couldn't look for any more excuses or run away from my calling. God wouldn't be asking me to do anything that He hadn't equipped me for. This thing was bigger than me, but it was time to put my hands to it. God had to make my discomfort unbearable, so I could get things moving. And right in the middle of all that confusion and upheaval in my life, my businesses were born – Red Door Empowerment, a nonprofit organization, whose purpose is to empower individuals to walk out of things holding them hostage, came into being. Through community outreach, workshops, and resources, such as support groups, hurting women were able to walk through Red Door, and walk on to deliverance. Frances Bailey Enterprises provides certified coaching and products to help women learn and apply strategies to overcome life obstacles, achieve their goals, and walk in purpose.

I was excited about developing my businesses, going back to school, and being a wife and mother. But I was battling a chronic skin condition, and I expected a lot of support. When my expectations weren't fulfilled, when I didn't receive any extra push, I felt like giving up. However, I had to pick my head up, pat my own self on the back, and keep it moving. I had a vision, and lack of support wasn't going to be a distraction to me.

So, I had to start walking by faith. Speaking healing over my body and making declarations that my chronic condition was no longer going to have the best of me, I began to work. I would hold coaching sessions with my clients while in my bed if I couldn't get out of it. I even remember limping to an event my organization held, because I had to keep going. . . by any means necessary. I recall many nights attempting to bathe my children with tears running down my face because I could only use one arm and hand. However, the job had to get done, and this condition wasn't going to take away my motherly or wifely duties. My children and my husband needed me. After all the hell I had been through, I knew nothing else in life was going to overpower me.

When it came to my homework, doubling up on assignments became routine for me, especially when I felt a flare-up coming. I had to sacrifice time with my husband and my children, but knowing the end result gave me just that much more strength. Yes, I felt weak at times, and that was okay. God's strength is made perfect in our weakness, so I made it through using His strength and not my own. I was able to humble myself before God to see me through.

None of my challenges were too hard for God to solve. Stress had me thinking that everything had to happen now, but my faith reassured me that everything would happen in God's timing. After being in business for a while, walking blindly, holding on to my faith in God, praying, crying, and seeking God, He finally sent a breakthrough for my family and me. My husband was given a new government job, which helped to put us financially back in a place of peace; our credit card debt was paid, and my co-pay for my medicine dropped to zero dollars, allowing me to be able to get my medicine. Being tested in those areas of my life helped me to discover my strengths, and my act of obedience to God to answer His calling was one of the very things that broke the chains of my financial struggle. God opened door after door for me that I had never imagined being opened. It felt as though my life was literally transformed from poverty to riches.

Reflecting on my life as a wife in business, I see there was purpose in all my pain. Being an entrepreneur has shown me that what the enemy uses to hurt you, God uses to prosper you. So, I encourage you to answer the call from God and stay close to Him even when you want to walk away from your relationship with Him because of life challenges. Use those difficult moments to dig deep within yourself and use your pain to birth your purpose and vision. Let all the distractions, such as bad relationships, sicknesses, and financial issues that are tossed your way, work for your good.

Remember, it's okay to feel broken, to be broken, just persevere to your calling. You may not have all the support you may want, but you must remember your purpose. Don't let go of your dreams and visions, and don't downsize or settle because they seem to be just fairytales. I'm here to tell you that fairytale dreams do come true. Through all the rough patches, I am walking the manifestation of the dream I had as a young girl.

There is something solid, uplifting, and inspiring about a woman who overcomes everything that was meant to destroy her. There is something divine about her when she begins fulfilling God's promises in her life. I am that woman. I am a resilient wife in business. And I am telling you that you are capable of being that woman in your own life, as well.

I Didn't See It Coming

Charlene W. Dozier

"But as for you, ye thought evil against me;
but God meant it unto good, to bring to pass, as it is this day,
to save much people alive."
~ **Genesis 50:20**

After recovering from a damaged and damaging 18-year relationship with my ex-boyfriend, I rededicated my life to Christ. I knew in my heart Sam was trouble, but it wasn't until after we had moved in together, six years into our relationship, that he told me he was a drug dealer. Gradually, his infidelity, lies, manipulation, along with mental, verbal, and physical abuse, drove me into a deep depression. I was hospitalized after a suicide attempt, and it was then I realized he never really loved me.

Through my mental breakdown, I realized my worth and knew I had to leave. I repented and asked God to help me from there on out. I dedicated my body back to God as a living sacrifice and declared that no other man would touch my body until he was my husband. I was healing from my toxic relationship with Sam and truly wanted God to step in and take the wheel. It was very obvious that me doing it on my own wasn't working, and I was tired of trying in relationships. I was seeking counseling and working to find myself. Understanding my worth was key to my process.

After five years of soul searching and not dating, I found myself growing stronger in my walk with the Lord. I continued building my faith up. My God-sister and I would pray together, and study God's word, and watch The Word Network for hours at a time each day. I'd review the different sermons and immerse myself in His Word constantly. My God-sister introduced me to a powerful woman she met years before, who was a Captain Intercessor, and someone she thought would be a great person for me to talk to while trying to heal from a bad relationship.

The three of us spoke on a three-way call, and it was like fire coming through the phone! She immediately invited us to come to NYC to her house, because she was having a prayer gathering the following Saturday. We were extremely prayerful along the ride, anointing our bodies with blessed oil. I tell you we were on fire for the Lord, and my goal was to seek him like never before. I finally realized that God had been with me in the previous relationship. As a matter of fact, He had been with me all my life, even while I was forming in my mother's womb. The Lord heard my cry all along.

So that Saturday, my spirit was leaping as we knocked on Mrs. M's door. She and my God-sister embraced very tightly, praising God, speaking in tongues, and rejoicing. Mrs. M's apartment was packed with a lot of praying, wailing women gathered together in fellowship. She introduced us to several ministers and prophets who were among us.

I was given a Scripture reading by Prophet Angela, who claimed she was moved to do so. My reading was Psalms 91, and that Scripture was so on point for what was going on in my life. I felt ministered to as never before. We couldn't even get interested in shopping in Manhattan, which we had planned to do afterward. Instead, we just kept walking and talking about the glory of the Lord we experienced in that apartment. Before we left, Mrs. M invited us to come back the following Saturday to go to a Powerful Women's Conference. The theme of that conference was "Women Fighting Against All Odds," and it sparked my spirit. What a statement to even think about!

The atmosphere was electric. As I was praying, all I could see were powerful women sitting with confidence and strength. The guest speaker took the platform, and I felt God's presence all over her. She preached my healing and deliverance on that day. She taught from the Book of Ruth:

> "And she said unto them, Call me not Naomi, Call me Mara: for the Almighty hath dealt very bitterly with me. I went out full, and the Lord hath brought me home again empty: Why then call ye me Naomi, seeking the Lord hath testified against me, and the Almighty hath afflicted me?"

That was the text she preached from, and I wept during the entire sermon. She was truly speaking directly to me. She proclaimed some of you are bitter because of the abuse you went through physically, mentally, and psychologically. You were in this relationship for a long time, and you ARE BITTER. But God ordained your steps to come here today to get your deliverance from the trauma you went through and kept secret. God said you're going to go home and clean out your closet from all the old stuff and start your NEW LIFE all over again. God is getting you in position for BOAZ is coming. I left the conference FREE.

This conference changed my life, and I realized then the importance of coming together with other women in a setting like this was so valuable.

I was attending the NYC church more regularly and was introduced to a fine young man who also attended. For the sake of my story and to protect his identity, I will call him "Mr. Secret." I was quite impressed with Mr. Secret. He was very articulate, good looking, and a servant of God. Months went by, and we were re-introduced to each other. I was shocked that he remembered me. Mrs. M arranged for us to have dinner. I was getting excited about my first official date after nine years of being clear from any men in my life, but I had to tend to my own business. It was the holiday season, and my mall kiosk business was in high gear.

We agreed to meet the following Saturday, and in the meantime, I had butterflies all week waiting for that day to arrive. We courted for a few months, but I kept having odd and peculiar thoughts about his 'friend.' On our way to the wedding of Mr. Secret's cousin, we made it official that we were going to be committed to each other in a relationship. I was excited to meet his family, and we had an awesome time celebrating at the cousin's wedding. I was treated just like I was a part of that family. At the reception, I never will forget they told me to get in the Family portrait with the entire family. I will TRULY say this was a very welcoming and loving family, down-to-earth, and authentic. I felt loved by them all.

I remember Mr. Secret telling me how he was working faithfully in ministry, and all his friends had married. He was the only one left with NO wife. He told me he realized God was sending him someone special. He told me God had ministered to him and advised him that I was a gift given to him, and he was to treat me with delicacy. I was honored and so happy because I was sure I had met my Boaz. He was the perfect gentleman, and we clicked automatically. I was honored that he was saving himself for his special bride, and I was doing the same thing. Every time Mr. Secret would hug me, I noticed his 'friend' seemed to be getting irritated. I even told Mr. Secret and asked if his friend was okay. He advised me to pay him NO ATTENTION, and so that is what I did. We agreed to date and travel to visit each other, so I would go to NYC every other weekend, and stay at the Hilton. We would go together to Mr. Secret's church on Sunday. We always got double beds and were careful about getting too physically close.

One time, we accidentally fell asleep in the same bed watching a movie. The next morning when we woke up, Mr. Secret stated we couldn't afford to sleep in the same bed together, which I agreed to, but it was truly an accident. But he made me feel so dirty, like I was trying to come on to him, and that was never the case. I truly LOVED him, but I loved God more. I loved God enough to do the right thing and wait on God's timing. I was so in love and just happy to be with someone who treated me like a Queen. It was any woman's dream to be in a relationship like this. He would surprise me with gifts of jewelry. We never argued or fussed. We shared our excitement to see each other, and we shared laughter, enjoying being in each other's presence. I will never forget on Valentine's

Day we were out at dinner. By candlelight, Mr. Secret got down on his knees in front of all the people in the restaurant, and proposed to me, asking me to take his hand in marriage. The people in the restaurant were clapping and excited. It was an unbelievably special moment, second only to the birth of my children. I cried as I said YES. I believed he was heaven-sent, and I was floating with the treatment I was receiving.

The Bible talks about being equally yoked, but Mr. Secret was such an awesome man of God. I knew God was going to bless his hands, and our marriage would be for ministry works, for sure. Shortly after we became engaged, Mr. Secret planned a special weekend for my birthday. We toured NYC on a boat and then checked into a beautiful, historic hotel in Manhattan. They gave us a tour of the hotel and then settled into our room with double beds, still honoring my wishes not to have intercourse until we got married. That evening, Mr. Secret took me to see "Phantom of the Opera" on Broadway. When Mr. Secret asked me what I thought about the show, I told him the main teaching is the love between two people cannot be forced. Every human has a desire to be loved. We continued to celebrate over dinner and walked through downtown Manhattan, taking pictures, and enjoying each other.

After nearly seven months into our engagement, during which time we were nearly inseparable, Mr. Secret advised me that the Lord said completion, and that we should prepare and plan our wedding ASAP. I was so excited that I ordered invitations the following weekend. Because Mr. Secret didn't have the money just yet, I charged them on my card, but we both agreed on the invitations, and he said to me, "Babe, I will pay you back." I didn't think anything of it.

I asked him about marriage counseling, which Mr. Secret scheduled with his Pastor. The marriage counseling session was over the phone, and for just one hour. But I was submitting to his wish, as he was the head in our relationship. I wanted more counseling, so I arranged several sessions with my Bishop. We learned a lot about each other, but maybe I didn't learn quite enough. Still, my Bishop emphasized the importance of the covenant relationship with God. A three-strand cord isn't broken with God in it.

In the meantime, I was going back and forth to NYC and David's Bridal, getting all of my wedding party's dresses situated: eight bridesmaids and one maid of honor. My colors were lapis and silver, and each lady would pick out a dress in a different design. We shopped around and visited over twelve different spots, but I was told as soon as you walk in, you will know the place to have our reception – and I did. It was The Davenport in New Rochelle. This place was amazing and the ideal place for a reception.

Days before my family was coming in, I stopped by the hotel to see the Cabinet Suite I reserved for our honeymoon weekend, and it was beautiful. I then stopped by Mr. Tuxedo to purchase my grandson's adorable tuxedo. Mr. Secret always operated with a spirit of excellence, and he refused for anyone to have to be stranded or rent a car unless they wanted to. So, he appointed himself to pick up a lot of his family members and the few of my friends coming in from out of town. Everything was falling into place as our wedding approached.

Our wedding rehearsal was great. We got everything organized, and everyone was filled with excitement for both of us. Afterward, we enjoyed our rehearsal dinner downstairs in the fellowship hall of Mr. Secret's church. I cooked all the food and was so tired, but with everything going on, sleep wasn't an option. And then my wedding day arrived. As I put on my dress, I told my sister, this was a love story God had created. The excitement started when my daughter and sister went down the aisle. The wedding march for me began to play, and my heart was racing with excitement. I was smiling from ear to ear walking down that aisle. I was thankful and grateful that God connected me to my Boaz, just like in the Bible. I waited nine years, consecrating my body, waiting for my Boaz. This was the day that the Lord had made, and I would rejoice and be glad in it.

Vocalists sang "A Ribbon in the Sky" and "I Believe in Miracles." I stood before over 200 people as we were pronounced Mr. and Mrs. We walked together down the aisle, and they had a tunnel formed for us to walk through. The whole ceremony was breathtaking. After the ceremony, we loaded up the wedding party in the Party Bus, and we were off to the reception. When we arrived, people were enjoying hors d'oeuvres and drinks. It was just a wonderful atmosphere of fellowship and getting to know each other. Everyone who came stayed 'til the end and guests commented over and over that this was the best wedding they had ever attended. All of the planning and excitement that went into my wedding day, and my fairytale love story ended abruptly after being married for only six months. There were signs, but I had my blinders on. As I reflect on it, I thought and felt God had sent me my Boaz, but I never actually asked Him about it. I just assumed it to be true because of the way things unfolded, fairytale-like.

I realized something was wrong when we never consummated our marriage. All I could do was pray. When I asked him if he took an interest in men, he said yes, as though it were nothing to reveal. The next morning, he waited until I had gone to work, then packed up all his things – including all the many things I had bought for him – and left. I was confused, yet oddly relieved. But I was also sad and broken. Again, during that short marriage, I internalized a lot of things. He wasn't affectionate toward me, so I wondered if I was attractive. I questioned my self-worth, which impacted my level of confidence. I went through extensive counseling to find myself again, and to deal with the root of it all. I still needed to figure out who I was as a woman, and even who I was as someone's wife. I found myself back at square one, and it was at that time the Lord revealed to me that I was a Woman Destined with Purpose, despite this love story gone bad.

Although the idea about my business came while I was married, and although I shared it with my then-husband, it wasn't birthed until after the divorce. It is my charge to help women who are seeking to find their destinies, especially those who are stuck and feel lost. As wives, we internalize a lot of stuff, and some stuff doesn't even belong to us. But we hold it, we keep it, we nurture it, we breathe it, and we bury it. Most times, we don't even deal with it. Part of what I was feeling and sensing about Mr. Secret's "friend" turned out to be true, and that's why our marriage ended so soon and so abruptly.

Of course, I was devastated, but I have learned that I need to seek God through the good times and the bad times. Everything that glitters ain't gold, and if we are seeking God with questions, we must be ready to receive the answers.

Don't give up on your purpose. Make sure you have connections and relationships that will support you. Make sure your foundation (YOU) is built on a solid rock (Christ)! I didn't see it coming, but I am resilient. And this story has a Part Two!

Finding the Right Balance

Lashonda Wofford

"Your dream was given to you. If someone else can't see it for you, that's fine, it was given to you and not them. It's your dream. Hold it. Nourish it. Cultivate it."

~ **Les Brown**

Often, I am asked how I built a successful business while being an engaged wife, mother, and grandmother. My answer is always: God, my husband (my rock), my immediate family, a lot of prayers, tears of joy and frustration, and plenty sleepless nights.

For years I dreamed about owning my own business, but that dream quickly became something I had to do, because I had no other options. But I didn't want to own just any kind of business; I wanted to own my very own home healthcare business. Home health care is very near and dear to my heart because of my experience with my first husband, David, who was robbed, shot, and left for dead. I cared for him in the comforts of our home for seven years. During those seven years, I learned so much, good and bad. The love and compassion that I had for David are what fueled my passion for stepping into the home healthcare industry. I took all the things I learned about caregiving, all the things I observed as a client, all the things I liked – and disliked – and used them as the foundation to build my business. I realized that so many other individuals and their families needed the same things that David needed.

David required around the clock care seven days a week; he required extensive hands-on assistance with day-to-day things such as bathing, grooming, and dressing. These were all a part of the daily hygiene routine for him. He also required a lot of medications and tube feedings throughout the day and night to help with his overall health.

Caring for him was so hard at first, and it was also very intimidating, but I was determined to do whatever I had to do to keep my family together. After the first few months, things become so much easier, like second nature. The hardest part of all of this was learning the ins and outs of the ventilator, which was also the most important part, as this was the one piece of equipment that he needed to sustain his life. Even though he had been approved for twenty hours of skilled nursing services seven days a week, I found myself without coverage five out of the seven days. It got to the point that I didn't even sleep in my bed. Instead, I would make a palette on the floor in his room next to his bed just in case the vent alarmed, or he needed oxygen, suctioning, or anything else.

It was impossible for me to work or finish college because I never had coverage. On the days when I thought I had coverage for him, I would make plans, but no one would show up, and often the agency wouldn't even call to let me know that no one would be there. Eventually, I stopped making plans ahead, but instead,

I would plan my day after the nurse showed up for work. There were so many times I had a nurse show up to work, but they were not competent enough to care for him, and would not have any experience with trach or vent patients, so I would send them home and call the agency to put them on the do not return list. I couldn't understand why the agency continued to send inexperienced nurses to our home to care for him.

Needless to say, I eventually switched to another agency. No agency can guarantee coverage twenty-four hours, seven days a week, but at least the new one tried and communicated with me in advance when shifts couldn't be covered. Once tragedy strikes, a good home health agency, and great care provided by compassionate and capable individuals can change the quality of someone's life for the better, regardless of diagnosis or prognosis. Doctors never expected David to live past twenty-four hours, and he lived for seven years.

On March 7, 2007, he gained his wings. This was so hard for me, and for years I blamed myself. What started as a routine ride via non-emergency transportation by Emergency Medical Staff to the emergency room for chest x-rays and antibiotics ended his life. Individuals with trachs and ventilators are prone to pneumonia, and David was no exception. I knew the signs and symptoms, so I would call the doctor and get a verbal order from her to take him in for chest x rays, blood work, and antibiotics. I could not ride in the ambulance with him this time, because I didn't want to get stuck at the hospital and not make it back home to get our baby, who was only eight years old at the time, off the bus. So, I decided to drive behind the ambulance. Worst mistake of my life. He passed away en route to the emergency room, but no one would admit it at first.

Building my business while being married wasn't the hardest thing I've ever done, but it certainly had its challenges. Before my current husband and I were married, we discussed our dreams and goals with each other. I told him in full detail about my dream of wanting my own home healthcare agency. He knew the passion that I had for it, and he knew my WHY behind all of it as well. As the years went by, the conversation would frequently come up, but no effort or action came behind it. It takes a lot of money to start an agency, and while I was willing to sacrifice to make it happen, my husband wasn't. Whenever the conversation came up, I would ask about the money for application fees or startup expenses, and my husband's response was consistently "we don't have it" or "we can't afford to do that right now."

I stopped asking, and I started feeling as if my husband didn't believe in or care about my dream, and that caused a big issue, especially because I had made my goals so clear to him. I became upset and angry with him, and I allowed little things that he did to make me so mad. I became so sad, frustrated, and unhappy, and it felt like my marriage was failing. We couldn't even stand to be around each other. Neither of us had the energy to argue anymore, but we knew it was going to happen. It was so ridiculous! Small things would turn into huge arguments, and most of the time, after the argument was over, we couldn't even remember the cause of it.

I loved my husband, but I was angry with him for what felt like lack of support and I was frustrated because I felt like he had become content with just being mediocre or average, and was no longer willing to support me in making my dream come true.

The frustration then turned into sadness as I started to second-guess everything about my marriage. I couldn't understand why my husband wasn't helping me when this business was for us, for our kids, and for our family.

One day, my husband suggested – as he frequently did – that we sit down together to write our five-year plan, to include our personal and professional goals and the plan to get them done. This made me livid! I wasn't going to continue to have these meetings and conversations when nothing ever came out of them. I demanded to know the point of having these so-called five-year planning meetings when afterward, nothing happened, and nothing changed. This definitely caused a big argument.

As I remember, this one was really bad, and things got way out of hand. My husband is a talker, so he believed that we should talk through our problems, no matter what. But I am the total opposite. I shut down when I'm upset because I prefer to process my own thoughts and feelings first. I don't like to talk about things while I'm upset or mad because I never want to say something out of anger to hurt my husband that we can't come back from after the argument is over. Anyway, this particular day he wouldn't let it go. We were going to talk about this.

My husband looked at me with tears in his eyes and said, "Baby, let's talk about it. I didn't get married to be unhappy or to get divorced. This is forever so we have to fix it!" "You look at me like you hate me," he continued. "You're so unhappy, and I need to know how to fix it."

At that very moment, I knew that my actions had hurt him, and I never wanted that. Through tears, I explained to him that I didn't feel like he supported me and my dream. He didn't believe that it could happen. All he thought about was working hard for other people. "If we're working so hard making other people's dreams a reality, we're never going to have time to work on ours!" I cried.

My husband looked at me and said, "Baby it's not that I don't support you or believe in you because I do. You're the hardest working woman I know! Your drive and passion are insane, and I envy you sometimes because you are such a go-getter. But Akins is your dream. I don't know the first thing about home healthcare and can't have the same level of passion you do. It's your dream. I didn't experience the things you went through with David. I'm here to support you, but you have to take the lead on this, and I will assist you. You have to tell me exactly what to do and how it needs to be done." Then he added, "I'm never going to take money from this household to fund a dream, not even mine. We will wait to get ourselves in a better financial place, and when we can move money to start the business, we will."

This opened my eyes so much because I never once considered the fact that he didn't understand home healthcare the way I did. He hadn't had the years of experience as a client and as a manager in the home healthcare industry. And he was right: Akins was my dream. I felt horrible because I never once considered any of this. I apologized, of course, because I had been the cause of so many arguments by coming to my own conclusions and not communicating clearly with my husband. Once I realized and understood this, my stress level went way down. I started working on the plan that I had written out years prior to meeting my husband, and when I needed his help with something, I would explain it and tell him and provide examples on how to get it done. It was so unfair for me to expect my husband to have the same passion and the same know-how as I did.

I look at him now, and I appreciate him so much for just being honest and telling me the truth. It forced me to reevaluate myself, and honestly, I hadn't really put in the work to make my dream a reality. I realized I had been looking to him to make my dream come true for me, and how crazy is that? How could I expect my husband or anyone else to work on my dream if I wasn't also willing to do so? I promised myself I would never make that mistake again. No one would ever work harder for me than I work for myself, and I would never work harder for someone else than I do for myself. Lesson learned!

When things got overwhelming for me, I would just take a deep breath, and take on one task at a time to get it done. I created timelines and set deadlines to achieve each goal while taking things one task at a time. Still, I had a hard time finding the balance between grinding it out and working my business, working a job, being a wife, a mother, and grandmother. Time management was definitely a struggle for me. I would get focused on something, and I would stay at the office day and night if I felt like I had to. On the nights I would order pizza for the kids from the office, my daughter would call, asking, "Hey Mommy, are you still at the office? What time do you plan on leaving?"

Many days my husband would get off work and call me to find out what we were eating for dinner, and I would have no clue because I was working. After a while, he stopped asking, and would just get off work and go to the grocery store to get something to cook. I remember one day I asked him what he wanted because I was at the grocery store, and he said, "Baby, I got something for today yesterday!" He said, "don't get me wrong, I admire you for your hard work and dedication, but you have to learn how to turn that off!"

I became concerned because it felt like my family had learned how to function without me. I was continually disappointing them. I had to switch gears quickly, and once again, lesson learned, new habits formed. In this way, my husband became my voice of reason. When I got too narrowly focused on something, he helped me see the larger picture. Because of his perspective and ability to see beyond the present moment, I came to trust his judgment. I had to retrain myself and my way of thinking. I just had to take a deep breath and allow my husband to hold my hand as we took this journey together. I had to learn to trust and respect my husband and the decisions that he made for our family and our business.

Through these challenges, our marriage has gotten stronger, because at the end of the day we know we each come first for the other. I often thanked God for my husband. We are a team no matter what, and his number one priority is to make sure we're good. That has always been his priority, though it took a few years for that to click in my head and my heart.

Now we have set office hours, and that's that. I'm not at the office outside of our designated business hours. Every now and then I may have to be there on a Saturday but not often and he understands that. I no longer take time away from our family to work. I'm present for my husband. I'm able to take our grandson to school and pick him up in the afternoon. I spend time with our daughter and make time for my son when he comes back home to visit. Sometimes as entrepreneurs, we can't see when we're asking our loved ones to sacrifice more than they're willing or should have to. They want us to be successful, but they also want us to be present in their lives.

Once my husband and I were in a better place and building a solid business, I fully expected my family and close friends to show up and support me, but that wasn't the case. I found myself dealing with the same anger and frustration all over again, but this time towards my extended family and close friends. I remember saying to myself, I am the first person in my family to have this type of business – a business that would create generational wealth, create jobs in our communities, and set the tone and trajectory for the lives of our children, and their children! Why were they not showing up and supporting me?

I knew that this was my dream and not theirs, but it still hurt when they failed to show up and support me. I couldn't even get them to make a simple referral or share a social media post! They would go work for another agency or refer a client to another business and then casually say, "Oh I didn't even think about your agency."

One day, as I was driving to a meeting, a family member called and asked for a loan. I became so emotional that I hung up the phone with angry words and tears of frustration and hurt. I knew I had to do something to shift this negative energy. Desperate for anything, I seized on a recorded motivational speech and started listening in my car. I stumbled on the words I needed to hear, as the speaker said, "You're upset because your friends and family don't support you, your dreams, and your business. Don't be," he said. Then, he explained why:

> "Most people, including our friends and families, don't have big dreams, or if they do, they're too afraid to go for it, or they don't know how to dream big. It's unfair for you to expect them to believe in something that seems so big. If they can't see it for themselves, what makes you think they can see it for you? Most people can't believe in something until they can touch it, and everyone is talking about it."

WOW! This random motivational speech changed my life because I had never looked at it this way until that moment, and for me, it made all the sense in the world. At that moment, my mindset shifted. I realized that I had to learn how to redirect my thoughts and emotions so that I could continue to do what God called me to do. My family and friends were off the hook. I no longer expected them to understand and do things as I did. I had to get in my own zone and realize what God gave me, trusting that he would provide. God has sustained us this far, and I know he will continue. Every time I have a negative thought, I can hear the words of that speech in my head. I thank God for the opportunity to examine myself through personal development. It helped me to push past the feelings of anger and frustration.

Personal development is still a major part of my life. I dedicate time every morning to listen to motivational speeches because they keep me focused and open my eyes to view situations and people in ways that I normally wouldn't, all while continually grooming me into becoming the best version of me. I will not hold people to standards outside of their abilities, because it's unfair to them. I love and appreciate all my family and close friends, but my dream is my dream, and I understand now that God gave me the vision, and I trust that He will surround me with the right people to support that dream and help make it a reality. My husband and I will continue to build a legacy and generational wealth for our family. I will continue to show up every day, pushing past all obstacles to change the lives of our clients.

My advice to other wives, mothers, and grandmothers who want to become entrepreneurs is to ignore your fear, write your plan down, and work on it daily. Don't expect your husband to share the same amount of passion for your dream as you do. Allow him to help in a capacity within his limits. Remember that support comes in many different forms, and it may not look exactly the way you think it should.

Don't allow your business to take too much time away from your family. Don't ask your family to sacrifice too much as you're building your dream. Don't spend time and energy worrying about your family and friends not supporting you. Just keep building. You have to believe in your dream before you can convince anyone else to believe in it. And don't expect anyone to work on your dream harder than you do.Show up every day in some capacity in your business, in your family, and in your own life.

Empty Arms

Effie Robertson

"Bad things do happen. How I respond to them
defines my character and the quality of my life. I can choose
to sit in perpetual sadness, immobilized by the gravity of my loss,
or I can choose to rise from the pain and treasure
the most precious gift I have – Life Itself."

~ **Walter Anderson**

I screamed out in excruciating pain as the nurse stood next to me, yelling at me to push my baby out. The contractions were coming so hard and fast that I began hyperventilating. I was exhausted and mentally drained.

An epidural was not an option since she was coming so fast, which left my body in a state of unbearable agony. I desperately looked to my husband for guidance and strength. I squeezed his hand tightly in hopes of providing myself with some type of relief from the pain that was overtaking my body. As I gazed into his eyes, what I saw was the joyful anticipation and excitement of the birth of our baby. I was so excited for him. I had experienced the most wonderful pregnancy through his immense amount of love and attention he bestowed upon me.

Knowing that he would be a wonderful father to our baby provided me with a sense of peace and furnished my body with a renewed strength for delivery. I labored for approximately twenty minutes before my princess made her grand entrance into the world.

My baby's cries echoed softly in the cold hospital room. Her cry was so faint that I struggled to hear her as I looked past the doctor toward the nurses, who frantically took her away from me. I immediately knew, from the depths of my soul, that something was catastrophically wrong. She did not deliver a strong, bellowing cry like my son did when he was born just two years prior. Instead, it was soft, like a gentle plea for help. A weak, little cry to let mommy know she was here, but everything wasn't ok. I began screaming, "Give me my baby! Let me see my baby!" I bellowed again, "please give me my baby," as my voice began to trail off, and heavy tears began to drench my face.

Almost instantly, all the frantic movement in the room began to slow down. There was an abrupt silence. My baby no longer cried her gentle cry. The sudden quietness in the room felt like a fifty-pound sack of heavy, wetted sand on my chest.

I screamed, "what's wrong?!" I could hear my own voice echoing in the cold, sterile room. I screamed again, "what's wrong with my baby?!" I heard my voice fading and drifting outside of my existence as I repeatedly requested to have my baby. I looked to my right as the doctor approached my bed, and clumsily removed his gloves from his hands. He couldn't even look me in my eyes. Instead, he looked down toward the floor and gripped tightly onto the bed rails.

The only words I remember him stating were, "I'm so sorry to have to tell you" before the remaining words drifted off in the distance.

I did not want to hear the ending to that sentence. I did not want to be a part of this ridiculous conversation. All I needed at that moment was for him to hand me my hungry, crying baby, while congratulating me on how beautiful she is. I struggled to witness the movement in the room as the pace and presence of each medical professional began to dissipate. Their intentional movement somehow was an indication they had reconciled with the reality of this situation. I began to feel unfamiliar with my surroundings and disconnected from anyone that remained present in the room. My environment appeared distorted, almost colorless. This was a dream! This was not the reality of my life. I was going to awaken from this horrible nightmare and walk out of this hospital with my baby wrapped in my arms. She would sleep in her new crib as the teddy bear mobile spun in a circular motion and hummed sweet lullabies.

One nurse remained within the room as everyone else retreated to their daily routines. The woman plodded across from her position in the corner to my bedside and asked if I wanted to hold my child. I emphatically stated "no" and asked her to leave. I turned towards the window and stared out in disbelief. I wanted nothing to do with this world, her, the swaddled baby, or my husband at this moment. I felt I couldn't safely and guiltlessly cradle my baby in my arms. What possible explanation could I give my little princess for her untimely death? What comforting words could I speak over her lifeless body to aid her in her transition? I didn't even want comfort from my husband. I felt guilty. Moments before, I reveled in the joy that beamed from his eyes from the anticipation of her birth. Now, I felt the need to explain why he would no longer feel that joy. How could I ever explain to him that I lost our baby? Now his eyes were empty like a black hole amid a massive rainstorm.

I wanted to go back to yesterday. I wanted to feel her kicks – her movement. I wanted to experience the horrible nausea that I endured for all those weeks. I wanted yesterday back. I wanted my baby back. Moments dragged by, or what seemed like hours when I took notice that the nurse continued standing off in that dark corner, just holding my swaddled baby.

Why was she still here in the room? Was she waiting for time to reverse itself? Was she waiting for God to miraculously appear and perform a miracle? I slowly lifted my head towards the nurse and stretched my arms out to receive my baby. I wanted – no, I needed – to see my baby. I un-swaddled her and laid her directly on my heart. I needed her to feel all the love that I felt and would always have for her. I wanted her to feel the warmth of my body as much as I needed to feel hers. I needed her tiny ears to hear me whisper how much mommy loved her. How much she was wanted, needed, and loved. I wanted her to hear how she would be forever missed. Most importantly, I wanted her to know how sorry I was that I couldn't save her. I couldn't fix her. I couldn't breathe life back into her. I needed her to forgive me for not having the ability to retreat into our yesterday and make everything all right for her.

The time a mother has to spend with their child, whether it's five minutes or fifty years before their death, is still just as precious and irreplaceable. The more years you have spent with that child, the more memories and experiences that haunt you daily. The less time spent with that child, the more cheated you are left to feel by the loss of future moments – and happiness that was promised to you.

Losing a child is so great that it seems impossible to go on living. Nothing in life feels the same or functions the same. It feels like an open, throbbing wound. There is no tourniquet, trauma dressing, or stitch that could stop this bleeding. This trauma will leave your mind in a state of disorganization and disorientation. I was shut down while being entrenched with feelings of being lost and confused. My sorrow was rooted in a period of absolute devastation. Days of grieving consisted of excruciating heartache, alternating with complete numbness. The vast emotions I felt ranged from disbelief to extreme anger.

Yes, I questioned GOD. Hell, many days, I sat in my car just screaming at Him and repeatedly asking why. . .why take my baby? Although I had another child to care for, any emotion or need beyond simply existing was lost to me. For a time, the death of my baby robbed me of my ability to carry out my parenting role as I imagined it should be. Along with my grief, I carried an overwhelming sense of failure. I failed my deceased child. And now, I was failing both my son and my marriage.

The death of our child did not strengthen our marriage; instead, it developed into a black hole that sucked our strength and consumed our every emotion. The first few nights at home comprised of sleepless nights. Eventually, every night seemed endless and fragmented with thoughts of guilt, questions, and wet pillowcases. We avoided one another. Many nights I could hear his quiet sobs alternate with mine. We were so deeply consumed with our personal grief that we each became disconnected and even disinterested in the depth of the other's sadness. Coupled with the anger, guilt, blame, and shame that we often felt, this led to a time of extreme isolation in our marriage. We retreated to grieving alone and not with one another. We indulged in senseless arguments and petty name-calling. Hitting below the belt comprised of a barrage of verbal insults that intensified our individual parental sense of failures.

The overwhelming sadness and isolation were shattering our marriage. We had failed our beloved little girl. Now we were failing one another and our son as his parents. As days, even months passed, the death of my angel created a profound sense of clarity for my purpose in the world. I became thankful for the nurse that had the wisdom and foresight to remain silently off in a corner of the room while holding my sweet angel. I believe she understood me forgoing the opportunity to hold her close to my heart would forever become a deeply regrettable decision.

The overpowering sense of compassion and empathy the nurse showed me had never been a part of my life outside of my immediate family before. The moment she walked out of my room with my silent baby cuddled close to her chest, I knew deep in my soul, I wanted to share that same compassion and empathy with others. I wanted to be a comfort for all those broken hearts, just as that nurse was to me. However, I realized before I could take any steps to help anyone, I needed to heal my own broken heart. I needed time to wrap my head around the events that had just taken place. I needed to find a reason to even want to live and move forward.

"If we take care of ourselves, we help everyone. We stop being a source of suffering to the world, and we become a reservoir of joy and freshness." ~ Thich Nhat Hanh

There was no rhyme or reason for any grieving process. No textbook, article, or advice will help fill the void you feel in your heart. For me, the grief manifested in waves, not stages. There were intense emotions that tumbled and fell altogether while often remaining intertwined. A thunderstorm of grief would sometimes rear its ugly head with an all-encompassing flood of tears for long periods. The downpours became less in intensity and frequency as the episodes gradually eased into more cycles of cloudy days. My first step was to seek counseling.

Consequently, my husband and I both decided to participate in individual therapy. We both required a judgment-free zone along with the anonymity to reflect and process our emotions. Approximately nine months later, we decided to participate in couples' therapy. Our individual therapists agreed that we needed to continue jointly in order for our treatment, healing, and behaviors to become somewhat symmetrical in the process.

Since we both still desperately wanted our marriage, compartmentalizing our feelings alone was no longer the best route for us to take. Make no mistake. It was difficult talking to one another without throwing the blame card. But we loved one another, and we worked diligently. Those endless nights that we once faced apart, we now embraced in one another arms as the tears softly soaked into our garments.

I began journaling. This became a safe space to write down my thoughts and feelings that I still sometimes found it difficult to verbalize. Letting go of the guilt was a difficult step in my healing process. The guilt I carried was not my friend. It did not protect me from the reality of the situation. This overwhelming sense of loss I felt was never determined by her short life span. Instead, it snatched hopes, dreams, and unrealized experiences that we would never share together. I wallowed in what should have been, never taking time to realize all the joy that remained in my life. The surviving child that still needed me. No matter how great my loss, or how deep my grief, life was consistently blazing forward and I needed to be a part of that. I needed to move forward for a child who needed a whole mother and a husband who needed a wife. Continuing to yield in this paralyzing grief and sacrificing my role as his mother, was no longer an option.

Secondly, I needed to stop blaming myself. I had to reframe my thoughts of myself. Every day I would sit and reflect on that day and days prior to the incident. Those judgmental thoughts of "I should have" or "Maybe if I had done" would often creep in my mind. It would be like a movie playing in my head over and over. Let's be very clear; there is nothing we can do to change the past. It's gone forever! We can't rewrite the script. However, what we can do is flip that negative thought and say something like, "I am so thankful I had the opportunity to feel her move and kick that morning." Just writing those thoughts on paper brought joy to my heart.

Now, I am not minimizing the strength it took to even get to that point. I allowed myself to scream, cry, and dive straight into my self-pity moments, but I never stayed there for long. I took my moments, and then I brushed my shoulders off. No matter how difficult, I continued to move forward so that my child's death would never feel in vain.

Concurrently, with this process, I needed to commit to myself and my family. Many days I felt hopeless – and useless – as a mother and wife. My prayer for a long time was to die. If I wanted life to be different, I needed to become completely committed to the healing process. Allowing my emotions to run their course was alright, as long as I celebrated the small victories, like happier days without tears, or the joy of hugging and kissing my surviving child every night before he went to sleep. Another significant process in my journey was searching for meaning in my child's death. No one, not even God, could provide a reason to satisfy my soul. I certainly wasn't receptive to the cliché 'everything happens for a reason.' So, part of that search involved my purpose and a commitment to that purpose. Becoming a nurse and being able to nurture and care for others as that nurse had done for me became part of that change.

I studied, obtained my degree, and worked up the ladder of success. Within my career, I broke down the stereotypical barriers that come with being a young, black woman. I was successful in my career, but most importantly, to me, I was successful in helping others. I allowed no one, not even myself, to be robbed of my God-given potential and ability to serve others. I became a greater version of myself. Making the conscious decision to change my life no matter what difficulties was a necessary change. My narrative changed from bleakness to determination.

I had no preconceived notions that all would be easy. I was confident that roadblocks and failures would present themselves at every fork of the road. Nevertheless, I choose to outline and map out new chapters in my life. I allowed myself to surrender my heart to the present while allowing the assassination of the past and becoming a victor in my future. Showing up every single day for myself, and my family became a necessity, not an option. I had to be the best possible me.

So, I encourage you to never give up on yourself. Discard the words 'doubt' and 'impossibility' from your vocabulary and show up each and every day with certainty and possibility. Stop trailblazing on excuses and fulfill your purpose. Just start where you are. Believing in yourself is the key to living your authentic life.

"When your life is on course with its purpose,
you are your most powerful."
~ Oprah Winfrey

Today, I am appreciative and grateful for the bond that I created with my baby girl for those nine months we spent together. Memories of her will always be a reminder of the love within me and the love that I continue to share with the world. This life-changing event showed me a new way to love, new things to find joy in, and new ways to look at the world. The moment I looked at her beautiful face, I knew I would never fail another child. I would hear every cry, every laugh, and be present for any monumental moment. I knew I would be my best, do my best, and become the best version of me. Many days it felt impossible, but I managed to find happiness and purpose in my life again, and so can you. No matter how great the loss, there can be happiness again. You can find new ways of love, new things to find joy in, and new ways to look at and participate in the world.

This tragedy left an imprinted watermark within the depths of my soul. And although we may not choose every lot in life, we can choose to move forward from any circumstance. The most important legacy I will leave is not how many people that were inspired by me, but how many people I helped become more excellent versions of themselves.

Granting Grace to Self

Catherine Latoya Grant-Alston

"God, grant me the serenity to accept the things
I cannot change, courage to change the things I can,
and wisdom to know the difference."
~ The Serenity Prayer;
by Fred R. Shapiro

"Living one day at a time; enjoying one moment at a time; accepting hardships as the pathway to peace; taking, as He did, this sinful world as it is, not as I would have it; trusting that He will make all things right if I surrender to His Will; that I may be reasonably happy in this life and supremely happy with Him forever in the next. Amen."

~ Reinhold Niebuhr (1892-1971)

As I lay in the bed, awakened by my 6:00 AM alarm clock, I knew the day had come. I didn't want to do it anymore. "It" was life. I didn't have any more strength.

6:15 am... 6:30 am... 7:00 am... time just passed, and all I could do was lay there. I tried to rationalize with myself like I had done other mornings. "You can't give up; you can't be selfish." It just didn't work.

OK, let me try to pray. Whew! Jesus, where do I start? You know my life, I mean you are God so...ugh. I could feel myself getting upset because if God was God, and He controlled all things, then why did I feel like this? Why did I have such pain and emptiness inside? Why did He let me go through so much pain? I could feel my husband, Reggie, tossing and turning, and I knew he would be up soon. The kids would be up soon. I needed to get a move on it. "Get up!" I told myself, "you don't have time for this s*** today!" Nope, it didn't work.

Reggie, my husband, got up and went to the bathroom. When he came out, he said, "Bae, you OK?" I mumbled, "I'm not feeling too good." He said, "OK, you rest. I got the kids."

I didn't have the guts to tell him that I wanted to give up. Well, truthfully, I didn't want to look weak and vulnerable. I heard our son, Quincy, get up. As usual, he was coming to give Mommy a big hug and morning kiss. Reggie stopped him and said, "Mommy is not feeling well, so we are going to let her rest. You're hanging with Daddy this morning." I thought, oh, OK, cool, Daddy got this. I didn't have to force a smile to my little one, and more importantly, lie when he asked what was wrong. The reality was that I didn't have an answer to the question.

I could hear Reggie talking to the kids about school. Asia wanted to play the cello, and Reggie said it was OK. Quincy brought home a paper to sign up for football and was extremely excited. Reggie handled everything by picking out their clothes, preparing breakfast, packing lunches, and was heading them out the door.

So, they would be straight without me, right? I mean, he was a wonderful father. OMG, what was I thinking and why? I mean, I wasn't contemplating suicide, exactly, but I definitely wanted to run away. Of course, I wasn't going to do that. So then, what the heck was I going to do? Reggie had taken the kids to school and already returned. I could hear his footsteps coming up the stairs, and I was dreading the convo. I knew he was going to ask what was wrong and what could he do to help. I didn't really want to talk. I didn't want to go through a plan of what would make me feel better. I didn't want to talk about my stresses and how he could relieve them. Nope, none of that!

As he opened the door, I lay there, anticipating the conversation. He looked at me and said, "Bae, I think you should call Nayda." Wait. What? I softly replied, "Why you say that?" What he said shocked me. He said, "You've been in the bed for two days, no shower, barely eating, and you keep saying you don't feel good. I know you, Bae, and I think you should call Nayda."

Nayda was my therapist.

Reggie was watching me and patiently waiting for the time to say something. Two days? Get out, really? I hadn't realized it. He hugged me, kissed my forehead, and told me he was going downstairs to get his laptop so he could start working. He was going to be working from home today.

When he left the room, the first thing I thought was, get up and wash your behind! I had to think – two days, was he exaggerating? I looked at my phone and had 12 missed calls and 42 unread text messages. Holy Christ, how could this be? I got up and went to take a shower. My natural hair was matted under my bonnet. My nails were chipped, and my heels were ashy. My Goodness! I had to get myself together. I mustered up enough energy to get in the shower, brush my teeth and tongue, and put on some lip balm. Huntey, my lips were cracked and dry! I went downstairs to talk to my husband. At this time, guilt had set in, and I felt horrible for leaving him out to dry for two full days. He was on his laptop and looked up to see me. He smiled and said, "Hey, beautiful."

I smiled back and said, "Hey, Bae, you got time to talk?"

* * *

To understand how I got to this point, I need to look back and look deeply into my early life. I grew up on the North End of Hartford, in a housing development called the Nelton Court projects. As long as I could remember, I loved being in the projects. Everyone was family. I loved the water fights in summer and sledding down the hill to Main Street in the winter. I remember playing double dutch and slap boxing.

In the projects, I stayed with my cousin, Tee, but I went to school in East Hartford, where my grandmother lived. The notion was East Hartford had a better education system. I would go to school, and then my Uncle OG would bring me to my big cousin Tee's house when I got off the bus.

Tee and I had a special bond. She would always welcome me into her home and make me feel so special. Although she had a son, Boop, who I called my little brother, she made it known I was her favorite girl. I can even remember her standing in the kitchen at the stove with her favorite jeans on. The white ones with the color patch in the front. She had jeans with different color patches. I remember orange ones, and red, and lime green, among others. It was true fashion back in the 90s, but it was her fashion, too, colorful and bright.

Tee would always cook my favorite meal, which was white rice, fried corn, and chicken. Every day she would talk to me, ask me how I was feeling, and make fun of my proper pronunciation of words by calling me "white girl," but it never felt like a bad thing. She was proud of me.

My mother was a drug addict. She was often in and out of jail. Tee would sneak to bring me to visit my mother when she was in a halfway house. She would tell me that my mom was going to get better, and everything would be OK. I believed her because she was like my second mom. I remember the look on her face one day when leaving my mom. She told me to always love my mom because she loved me despite her addiction. Her look seemed sad. I didn't understand that look until I got older. There was nothing that Tee wouldn't do for me. With her presence in my life, I didn't feel the void of not having my mother there with me daily.

When I was nine, my cousin Tee died. She died on June 21, 1993, a day after she celebrated her 23rd birthday. Her son, Boop, had tried to wake her up, but she wouldn't move. He was trying to wake her up to bring him to school. I remember that day like yesterday. My grandmother put my friend and me in the car, and we went over to Tee's house. We still had on our pajamas. I wasn't old enough to understand death.

At the funeral, seeing her body in the casket made me scream and cry until I lost my voice. I remember my family carrying me out of the funeral home. My Aunt had the body transported to South Carolina for burial. I traveled but didn't have enough strength to go to the burial. It took me 15 years to visit her grave.

As I got older, I was able to understand what happened to Tee leading up to her death. A heavy box fell on her head when she was walking in the store. My Aunt said she appeared to have an altered, glazed look, but Tee said she was ok. From that day, she started to have seizures. Although she was put on medicine, it didn't really help. She had a seizure in her sleep the night she passed away.

Up until that time, I never felt a pain like that before. I knew my life would be different, but I didn't realize how much different. Every time I went to the projects after that, it didn't feel the same. I felt empty inside. I lost my cousin, my second mom, the only person that would take me to see my mom. It was like I lost two mothers at the same time.

I was getting older, and another one of my uncles, Do Right, didn't want me to be in the projects anymore. He would literally fight me (tough but no injuries) until I ran off. I started trying to sneak in the projects by going through a small path from Main Street, but Do Right would still see me. It just became worse each time he caught me. I ended up not going back altogether. It wasn't the same, anyway, and I honestly didn't feel like fighting off my uncle. I found out later that my uncle strategically did that to keep me out of the projects. He knew things that I couldn't see at that time. He knew that it was drugs, guns, gangs, and fast girls. He didn't want me involved in any of it. I'm happy he protected me from those things, although he could have just talked to me. But he did it his way.

As the years went on, so many of my old friends became drug

addicts, went to jail, became pregnant, or became prostitutes. Uncle Do Right's tough love was purposeful. I stayed with my grandparents in East Hartford all the time, and only made trips to the projects with my grandmother or Uncle OG. Uncle Do Right was fine when I was with them.

My mom was still in and out of jail, and her drug habit had gotten a lot worse. Every time she came around, it was empty promises. She always would ask to wear my jewelry but then wouldn't come back with it. She would pawn my rings and even pawned my boyfriend's chain. That was one of the few times I was embarrassed by her addiction. Even though she would do those things, seeing her was like having dessert for dinner. It was rare and wonderful and sweet. However, as I was getting older, I noticed it was detrimental to her health, and to my mental stability.

School became a place that I loved. Math was my favorite subject. I also discovered my love for double dutch, dancing, and step team. I actually felt like everything was going to be ok. But I was wrong. My grandmother worked at a prominent manufacturing plant in East Hartford. Her schedule got changed to the 2nd shift, which meant she worked from afternoon to midnight (or later sometimes). My grandfather worked 3rd shift at another manufacturing plant. My mom was home and living with us, but she would go missing for several days on drug binges. When the shift changes occurred, she assured my grandparents that she would be home to take care of me. I remember one night I woke up in the middle of the night. I couldn't sleep. I went to the basement to tell mom, but she wasn't there. She was nowhere in the apartment. I was scared and just went back up to my room. Somehow, later that week, my mother got caught leaving me in the house.

Life as I knew it changed again. I ended up going to stay with my cousins (who I didn't know were family at the time), and their mother, who I call Auntie. I went from having my own bedroom to sleeping on a cot in between two beds in my cousins' bedroom. They were great taking me in, but it wasn't home. I must admit, most days were fun. It was like living with siblings. I never experienced such a thing because I was an only child. We would laugh, joke, play, and fight just like siblings. I stayed there for two years. I would be able to go to my grandparents' house on the weekends, sometimes. I learned to call Auntie's house my home. I remember Auntie's sister coming down to visit one day. As I was standing there, she asked who I was. My Aunt explained the situation, and her sister said, "She's going to be really messed up and need a lot of help."

Those words crushed me! She talked about me as if I wasn't standing right there. In her opinion, I didn't stand a chance at being successful, and based on statistics, she was right. It was at that time I made the decision that I was going to prove her wrong. I was going to prove everyone wrong about me being messed up.

I went through middle school and high school as an honor roll student. Yea, I got into some fights, but that was the most trouble. I was pleasant in my classes. I was a homecoming princess and prom queen in high school. I served on the student council and was junior class president. I was NOT going to be 'messed up.' I graduated high school as an honor student with 12 college credits and earned a full ride to UConn School of Business. I ended up taking a semester off because college was a different environment and hard to adjust to. Since I had no prior grades to prove my GPA requirements were met, I ended up losing most of my scholarships. I couldn't become a statistic because I had to prove everyone wrong. So, I got a job working at the bank full-time and went to school full-time.

It was difficult, but I did it. I graduated with a business degree, then went on to obtain my MBA from the University of Massachusetts. I got married, purchased a house, and we had our beautiful daughter, Asia, all by the time I was 26. That wasn't enough, though. I was still on this path of proving everyone wrong. I started ART Financial Solutions, LLC, in 2010 and went fulltime with the business. I was determined to leave a legacy to my children. They would never need to go from house to house or worry about any of the things I did growing up.

Unfortunately, entrepreneurship is HARD. My fear of being broke was too much to bear, because being broke meant struggle. Struggle meant defeat. And that would mean that everyone was right and that I was messed up. Nope, not happening! So I decided I was going to go back to work for a corporation. Not only did I go back to work for a corporation, but I also worked my way up to become a corporate executive. My financial expertise afforded me the opportunity to win not one, not two, but three prominent awards in the industry: Alexander Hamilton Award, TMI Treasury Team of the Year, and FIS Impact Award. I WAS CRUSHING IT! With all these accolades, no one could ever say I was 'messed up.'

Even in difficult times with my health, which included experiencing a brain injury, heart surgery, and a full hysterectomy all before I turned 35, I continued to push and strive for excellence. Don't get me wrong. . . it was difficult. I experienced the brain injury in November 2012. I woke up early like I did each morning to get ready for work. I remember putting on my underclothes, a tee-shirt, and my favorite slippers. Some of my work clothes were hanging downstairs in the basement near the washer and dryer. I put on my robe and headed downstairs to get my work clothes. As I started to walk off the first step, I fell HARD. I hit my head on every step going down to the door. There were about six or seven steps since we lived in a raised ranch house.

When I opened my eyes, I remember my husband looking at me and asking me if I was ok. I responded, saying yes. He told me we needed to go to the hospital. I didn't understand why he was making such a big deal out of the fall. I was fine, and I needed to get to work. What I didn't realize was that when I fell, hitting my head, I started to seize. My eyes were rolling in the back of my head, and I was completely unconscious. So, when my husband was saying I needed to go to the hospital, he was trying to maintain his composure, but he was afraid. He ended up calling 911. I remember the EMT folks going back and forth about whether they needed to call this in as a head trauma. They eventually called in to follow protocol. I remember the hospital cutting my clothes off while I was in the ER. There were many doctors that came in and out, but I didn't see Reggie.

Little did I know, he was battling the hospital personnel because they thought he pushed me down the stairs. They would not let him in to see me. He finally told them he was calling his lawyer, and they would be sued if they performed any procedures on me without proper consent since I was not mentally capable at that time. As a result, they let him into the ER room. The doctors sent me for an MRI, X-rays, and numerous blood tests. I had contusions on my ribs and back.

There were a series of therapy tests that I had to complete before being released. A cognitive therapist from the neurology group came and asked some questions. He asked a series of math questions, and I answered them incorrectly. My husband looked at me, and I looked at the doctor perplexed. They were basic math questions, and I had gotten them wrong. I was a math guru! There was no way that I would get any math question wrong. It was the start of many tests that eventually led to my diagnosis of brain injury. I had lost some of my short-term and long-term memory. I was put on bed rest with no TV or phone for a week, then rehabbed for 30 days. I recovered strong but to this day still have some episodes of short-term memory loss.

In 2016, I started a bootcamp workout routine. The workout sessions were for 20 minutes, but I could only last 5 minutes. At first, I just thought I gained weight and was out of shape. But by the third day, I was experiencing ongoing chest pains that didn't feel right. I decided I would go and get it checked out. My primary doctor completed an EKG and sent me home with muscle relaxers and a referral to a cardiologist. I had already been to three cardiologists beforehand since I had a heart murmur. All completed EKGs and said I was fine. I didn't want to go to another cardiologist, but something just said to go anyway. I arrived at the cardiologist, and of course, my EKG was normal. However, this cardiologist was curious (his words) to see why I had the heart murmur, so he sent me for an echocardiogram, a sonogram of the heart.

A couple of weeks went by, and I didn't hear anything back. Usually, that means that everything is ok, but I called for my results anyway. The cardiologist's admin said the doctor took my file with him on vacation so she couldn't give me my results. She would page him and return my call. I knew that there had to be something abnormal for a doctor to take a file with them on vacation.

Sure enough, I received a callback that the doctor was returning the next day and wanted me to come in right away. I was told I had a hole in my heart. It was a defect that I was born with, and it had grown. If I didn't close it, it would cause my heart to go out of rhythm, and I would die from a heart attack. I was numb! My Uncle OG was in a vegetative state because his heart went out of rhythm, and he had a heart attack. They had performed surgery on him, and the result was that he could not move, talk, and was unconscious. I couldn't bear seeing him like that.

At that point, it had been five years that he was in that physical and mental condition. I didn't want to die, but I didn't want to have a surgery that yielded results like my Uncle. The pain of seeing him like that was too much, and I never wanted my kids to go through that. I cried, screamed, and was mad at God. I was scared. Eventually, my friend said something that made me look at this situation differently. She said, "If it was me, I would have the surgery. I wouldn't want to be with my kids and have a heart attack that could kill me. That would be too painful for them."

I knew I had to have the surgery. In September 2017, at the age of 33, I had heart surgery. The surgery was successful, and I was on the road to recovery. At least so I thought. It wasn't long after that I experienced some major pain with my menstrual cycle. At first, my doctors thought it was related to the blood thinners I was on due to the heart surgery. However, once I stopped the blood thinners, the pain and bleeding worsened. The best way to explain it was like having a charley-horse cramp in your stomach and back that you can't relieve.

After having an ultrasound completed, I was diagnosed with a severe case of adenomyosis. The only option was to have a hysterectomy. I was fine with the decision since I had already had a double tubal ligation removal. Reggie and I had already decided we were not having any more children, as we were already blessed with a son and a daughter.

In October 2018, just one year after my heart surgery, I had a full hysterectomy. Of all the surgeries, the hysterectomy was the most difficult to recover from. It took me a full 12 weeks before I didn't feel pressure or bloated. I was eager to return to normal. I didn't rest because rest would mean I wasn't out achieving goals. That was more important in my mind than any physical recovery requirements. However, trauma has its way of rearing its head. While I thought I was proving a point, eager to get back to crushing it, I really was failing.

My relationship with my husband was strained because I was so dominant. I would talk in a toxic way to him and maneuver as if I were a single person. There wasn't anything that he could say to me, because it was my way and that was that. By my logic, I had gotten this far by myself, so clearly, I knew what I was doing. The reality was I didn't know how to be vulnerable.

Vulnerability to me meant that something was wrong. Of course, nothing could be wrong because that would mean that my aunt's sister was right, and I was messed up. So, as a result, I struggled with letting him lead. My business was awful. It became inactive. The fear of failure and rejection trumped my passion. I wasn't building the business I dreamed of because it became too overwhelming. I didn't want anyone to tell me that my product or service wasn't good enough, because that would mean that I wasn't good enough. It didn't matter how often someone said that my services were needed. There was this little voice in my head that had doubt. That doubt always showed up and overpowered my confidence.

Most importantly, I felt like I was failing as a parent. In my mind, I was going to be the parent that showed up to every game, cooked every evening, and read bedtime stories every night. I felt horrible when the work obligations increased, and I started traveling more often. Eating out became routine. Mommy couldn't make every ceremony, field trip, and assembly. OMG, I was failing! When the kids cried because I couldn't be at one of their events, it made me remember the times I cried when my mom was not present. It was the most horrible feeling I had ever experienced.

The non-stop running, and obligation after obligation had finally caught up to me. This was why I wound up in the bed for two days. At least, that's what I thought. But the discussion I had with my husband that morning changed everything. "Hey Bae, you got time to talk" are words that I will never forget saying because they released so much that I had suppressed for so long.

* * *

Our intimate discussion revealed several things. As a wife, I was not operating as a partner. I was trying to build an empire alone. My husband wanted to support me, but didn't know how, because

I was not making space for him to coexist in this world I created. He made it clear that he wanted to support my passion, but he was not interested in validating a phantom thought of proving everyone wrong.

He made it clear that I didn't have anything to prove to anyone and that I was enough as I was. Point. Blank. Period! He led with compassion and understanding, not judgment and criticism. We talked about parenthood and how I operated like a single parent. He expressed how he felt he had to insert himself to be present as a parent. Most importantly, Reggie told me the demands that I put on myself were unrealistic. Wearing the title of mother, wife, and boss did not come with a manual. There was not a set path to doing it right or wrong.

Reggie's words resonated with me. He opened the door for me to be vulnerable and express my fears, something I had never done in that capacity before. That vulnerability fostered the change in my mentality on business, parenthood, and marriage. He helped me realize that it was ok to get it wrong. I didn't have to be perfect. I could make mistakes, and it was fine. But most of all, he let me know - he made me believe - that I was not a failure.

My husband saved me! I walked away from the conversation with a level of peace. Was it that simple and easy? Absolutely not! It took work to create a new thought process. I called Nayda, but I couldn't get on her schedule right away. She was vacationing in Puerto Rico. She had retired and was only taking some patients here and there. I knew I needed something more frequent and on a schedule. I also knew that one person was not going to talk to me and solve all my problems. I started to revert to my fight or flight mentality. However, I knew where that got me and that it was not the answer.

Every day I got up and started with an affirmation. Each morning I would look in the mirror and quote the serenity prayer, each paragraph. For the next few weeks, I paid attention to my emotions. I wrote down what things made me overwhelmed, what things gave me anxiety, and what things made me happy. I talked to some of my closest friends and let them know what was going on. That was something I had never done before. They showered me with love and prayed with me.

I became more open with my husband in articulating when I felt overwhelmed. We worked on a plan to relieve some of the household stressors. I let him in and let him lead as the head of the household. I slowly but surely started to focus on my happiness. Most importantly, I didn't equate rest with not being productive. I realized that I felt like I always needed to achieve the next best thing or pursue the next goal. After soul searching for many months, it became evident that resting was a part of refueling the soul. Nayda continued to make herself available to me via phone, which helped tremendously.

Some days are better than others. Some days are just plain tough. There are still some fears, hesitation, and feeling overwhelmed, but I grant myself grace. You know what I do on those days? I take some time to relax. Instead of thinking about my task list, I reflect on my accomplishments. Instead of thinking about everything that went wrong that day, I think about the wins of the day. When you need to show up as a mother, boss, and wife, it's easy to get overwhelmed. When you put those stressors on top of traumatic experiences that haven't been dealt with, it becomes toxic.

Today, when you ask me who am I, I am not messed up, that's for sure. I am Catherine Latoya Grant-Alston, an executive, an entrepreneur, a published author, a mother, and Queen of the Alston Kingdom. I am educated with a Master of Business Administration degree. I own several businesses. But most of all, I am happy! To me, that's the most important adjective I love to use to describe myself.

My advice is to deal with all the trauma you've experienced. It is extremely true that your emotional baggage will hold you back. I was so busy trying to prove a phantom point to people that didn't even matter. It was all in my head. The only person I had failed was myself because I wasn't living a life that I considered happy. I wasn't enjoying the moments.

You can't stop time or get it back. Don't waste it stressing over something someone said, perceptions, or fears. Don't compare yourself to the next mother who makes all the games. Don't cry because you didn't get the contract for your business. They just didn't understand or weren't ready for your level of excellence. Don't soak in the argument with your spouse. IT IS ALL OK!

Take care of yourself. Understand that you are not alone. Get the help that you need. Counseling is a great way to deal with trauma and stress. Being self-aware and self-loving is not selfish! Grant yourself some grace. You are more than just a mother, wife, and boss. You are YOU first, and YOU ARE ENOUGH!

ABOUT THE AUTHORS

Tamara Mitchell-Davis

Tamara Mitchell-Davis is a bestselling and award-winning author, public speaker, wife, mother and CEO of TM Davis Enterprise, LLC. She holds an MBA and an 085 School Business Administrator Certification from the State of Connecticut. She is an adjunct faculty member in the Business Department at Asnuntuck Community College in Enfield, CT. Her published works include *#GoalGetter* and *Goodbye Fear, Hello Destiny*, available at Amazon and Barnes and Noble.

Awards include: 100 Women of Color (Class of 2017) for leadership and community service; ACHI Magazine Orator of the Year (2019); and Women of Elevation Triumphant Author (2019). Media appearances include Women of Distinction Magazine, Inquiring News, Making Headline News, and Voyage Dallas Magazine.

Tamara is an active member of Delta Sigma Theta Sorority, Incorporated and serves on an advisory board in the Hartford school system. She also volunteers in a fundraising capacity for juvenile diabetes and various cancer research organizations.

Tamara resides in her hometown of Hartford, CT with her husband and their children. You can connect with Tamara at info@theceowife.com or visit her website at www.theceowife.com.

Dr. Sh'nai Simmons

Sh'nai Simmons, commonly referred to as "Dr. Sh'nai", earned her M.A. in Community Counseling and her Ph.D. in Counselor Education and Supervision from Regent University.

She is a Licensed Mental Health Counselor in Florida. She is the co-founder and owner of Community Victory Family Services, Inc., a private group practice committed to providing superior mental health services, including telehealth options for international clients.

Dr. Sh'nai works closely in ministry with her husband and business partner, Taiwan Simmons, to reinforce the power, purpose, and passion of traditional marriages through The Get In Touch Network, and to fill community gaps through their nonprofit organization, Inside Reach Ministries.

Dr. Sh'nai is the devoted mother of two biological, two adopted, and countless spiritual children. She is committed to "helping people use what they have to get what they want." You can connect with Dr. Sh'nai at www.DrShnai.com.

Nicol McClendon

Nicol McClendon was born and raised in Hartford, CT. Nicol's love for writing came at a young age, and continued throughout high school, when she would pen short stories and poems that won awards and earned her many opportunities as a public speaker.

Following the murder of her first husband, Nicol found the strength to continue living through writing and traveling. Nicol became an author and entrepreneur when she published her first book, *It's My Story I Will Tell It: Pieces of Me*. She published a companion journal, *The Writers Journal: It's Your Story, Tell It* to provide a guide for deepening the healing journey by allowing others to release their stories through expressive and reflective writing.

Nicol is a mother and a wife who will inspire you to open yourself up and pick up the pieces by continuing to believe in pure love and remembering the deep joy in living. You can connect with Nicol on Instagram @authornicolmcclendon or visit her website at www.nicolmcclendon.com.

Tangie R. McDougald

Tangie R. McDougald is a wife, entrepreneur, and native of Hartford, CT. She is a Licensed Professional Counselor and CEO of Community Matters, LLC. She is certified as a trauma focused therapist, and works with children, teenagers, and adults.

Tangie attributes her success in marriage and business to her faith in God. She has overcome multiple socio-economic barriers, including teen pregnancy, homelessness, dropping out of high school, domestic violence, divorce and sexual assault, to name a few. These challenges have served as catalysts in her quest to help others. Tangie has served as a volunteer to assist and counsel women of sexual assault, domestic violence, and lobbied for legislative changes in the prosecution of these crimes.

She no longer questions why things happen in life, because she understands that "there is...no testimony without a test" (Kris Vallotton, Spirit Wars). You can connect with Tangie at www.tangiemcdougald.com.

Cherry L. Jackson

Cherry L. Jackson was born in St. Louis, Missouri, and raised in Pensacola, Florida. She holds an A.A. from Florissant Valley Community College in St. Louis. She received her Business and Travel Certificate from the Wilma Boyd School, and has traveled extensively, both domestically and internationally, as a former TWA Flight Attendant. She has been employed with Graybar Electric Company for the past 23 years.

In 2018, Cherry earned her Evangelist Missionary License. Her ongoing ministries include her congregation's Youth Department, Usher Board, Praise Team, Singles Ministry, and Marriage Ministry. She has a special place in her heart for coaching and mentoring women on how to be healthy spiritually and physically.

Cherry is married to Elder Richard Jackson. They have six children, and three beautiful, busy grandsons. You can connect with Cherry at jacksonof6@yahoo.com or on Facebook @ Cherry Jackson.

Frances Ann Bailey

Frances Ann Bailey was born and raised on the Eastern Shore of Virginia. She holds a B.S. in Criminal Justice with a concentration in management and administration and is currently pursuing her M.P.A. and is also a certified life coach, specializing in empowerment and executive leadership. Frances is the founder of the nonprofit organization Red Door Empowerment, and CEO of Frances Bailey Enterprises, LLC. Additionally, she is a member of the Board of Directors for the Eastern Shore Center for Independent Living.

Her organizational memberships include: Alpha Kappa Alpha Sorority, Incorporated; National Society of Leadership and Success; Phi Theta Kappa Honor Society; and ACHI Women Supporting Women Association, Inc. She has been awarded the "Iconic Woman" award and has been a Virginia nominee for the National ACHI Magazine "Woman on the Rise" and "Community Leader of the Year" awards. Media appearances include WESR Shore Daily News, Eastern Shore Post, "The Jacobby Show" on WSKY-SKY4 TV, Making Headlines News with NBA reporter Andre Johnson, Moving Beyond Life's Giants with Williams Weeks, and Power & Grace Leaders: Falling in Love with Purpose with Chavon Annette.

Frances is a wife, mother, and devoted member of Anointed Word of Deliverance COGIC. You can connect with Frances via email at info@francesannbailey.com, on Facebook at Frances Bailey and Red Door Empowerment, Inc, and on Instagram @FranAnnBailey.

Charlene W. Dozier

Charlene Wendy Dozier, affectionately known as "Tangy," is a native of Hartford, CT. She is an ordained minister and motivational speaker, currently pursuing a B.S. in Business Management, as well as an A.A. in Biblical Studies. She has 23 years in Executive Leadership to include Associate Director of VZW and Operations Manager at Altice USA before taking over the CT Region Retail Sales Team. Charlene is also the CEO of Women and Men of Destiny LLC.

Following her chapter, "I Didn't See It Coming," in this anthology project, Charlene is planning an Autobiography of her life, "*What the Enemy Meant for Evil, God Turned It Around for My Good.*" She considers it her personal ministry to seek out the rejected, broken-hearted, and lost to help them become what God would have them to become.

Charlene is a divorced, single parent with two children, and two grandsons, and lives happily in New Britian, CT. You can connect with Charlene at Wodestiny2018@gmail.com or on Facebook @ CW Dozier.

Lashonda Wofford

Lashonda Renee Wofford is a native of Goldsboro, NC. She is the Founder and Chief Administrator of Akins Helping Hands, a family-operated business providing in-home care. She runs the business with her husband, who serves as CEO.

Lashonda is also the founder of GRACE Community Outreach, Inc., a non-profit organization that helps feed and clothe the less fortunate, provides support for victims of childhood sexual abuse and their families, and provides support to individuals battling cancer. She is a faithful member of Grace AME Zion Church in Raleigh, NC, where she has actively led the praise and worship team and sung in multiple church choirs.

Following her chapter, "Finding the Right Balance," in this anthology project, Lashonda will be releasing a new book, *Pain Equals Purpose*, in 2020. In this book, she will share her personal story about her late husband David Akins, and how God revealed her purpose through her pain. She is currently pursuing a degree as a Registered Respiratory Therapist. Lashonda and her husband, Travis, have two children and one grandchild. You can connect with Lashonda on Facebook at Lashonda Wofford or visit her website: www.akinshelpinghands.com.

Effie Robertson

Effie Robertson is a nurse with over 20 years of experience, a public speaker, and life/empowerment coach. She has a M.S. in Management and a B.S. in Business Administration. She is the founder and CEO of All In A Day Transportation, LLC, a medical transport company and also owns and operates Guardian Angels Connect, LLC, which provides community-based, in- home health care and assistance.

Effie has extensive experience in leadership, team-building and business development, which she leverages to help new entrepreneurs build and grow profitable businesses. She specializes in multi-generational workforces, employee empowerment, and employee wellbeing. She is directly responsible for the start-up of three companies, each of which have exceeded annual revenues of $1.5 million. Additionally, she started a cleaning company that generated over $100k in revenue in its first year.

Effie's professional philosophy embodies authenticity, empowerment, and growth. She is passionate about helping people reach a deeper understanding of themselves and others, in order to form more meaningful interpersonal connections, and build lasting relationships. You can connect with Effie at www.Effie-Robertson.com.

Catherine Latoya Grant-Alston

Catherine Grant-Alston is an author, entrepreneur, and treasury finance executive for a Fortune 300 company. She earned a B.S. in Business Administration from the University of Connecticut, and an MBA from the University of Massachusetts. Catherine is the CEO and Co-Founder of ART Financial Solutions, LLC, specializing in strategic vision planning regarding finance, liquidity, and treasury technology.

Special awards and memberships include: Treasury Management International (TMI) Innovation and Excellence Corporate Recognition Award for Treasury Team of the Year; Alexander Hamilton Award for Technology Excellence; and FIS Impact Award for Corporate. Her volunteer service includes: Member, Delta Sigma Theta Sorority, Incorporated; Academy of Finance Advisory Board, East Hartford Board of Education; Co- Opportunity Inc.; The Village for Families and Children; Agape Fellowship Ministries; and COA Enrichment Program Director.

Catherine lives with her husband and two children in Connecticut. You can connect with Catherine at info@grantalston or visit her website at www.grantalston.com.